great violinists
david oistrakh
wolfgang schneiderhan
arthur grumiaux

discographies compiled by john hunt

Acknowledgement

These publications have been made possible by contributions or advance subscriptions from

Richard Ames
Yoshihiro Asada
Marc Bridle
Brian Capon
Robert Dandois
John Derry
Henry Fogel*
Peter Fülop
Jean-Pierre Goossens
Alan Haine
Tadashi Hasegawa*
Bodo Igesz
Rodney Kempster
Detelf Kissmann
Douglas MacIntosh
Carlo Marinelli
Bruce Morrison
Alan Newcombe
Jim Parsons*
David Patmore*
James Pearson
Ingo Schwarz
John Shackleton
Michael Tanner
Nigel Wood*

Stefano Angeloni
J.M. Blyth*
J. Camps-Ros
Edward Chibas*
Dennis Davis
Hans-Peter Ebner*
Nobuo Fukumoto
Philip Goodman
Johann Gratz
Michael Harris*
Naoya Hirabayashi
Andrew Keener
Koji Kinoshita
Elisabeth Legge-Schwarzkopf*
John Mallinson*
Philip Moores
W. Moyle
Hugh Palmer*
Laurence Pateman
J.A. Payne
Tully Potter
Tom Scragg*
Yoshihiko Suzuki*
Urs Weber*
Graeme Wright*

*indicates life subscriber

Great violinists: an introduction
The three solo artists whose discographies are presented here are some of the most requested by my regular subscribers. From among the countless fine violinists of the twentieth century we have David Oistrakh representing the Russian school, Wolfgang Schneiderhan from the Austro-German tradition and Arthur Grumiaux representing the renowned Belgian tradition – each with their own individual sound characteristics.

In a 2004 survey in *Gramophone* magazine it was Oistrakh whose name was invoked most consistently by a group of today's young virtuosi as being most representative of what the past century has to offer in standards of recorded string playing. His recorded performances form an important link with the history of Russian music, dedicatee as he was for works by Shostakovich and countless other composers. Schneiderhan had lengthy periods as concert-master of Austria's leading orchestras before deciding to remain with a solo career. His smoothly elegant production was specially suited to the seminal violin repertoire of Bach and Mozart, although he may have been heard less, with certain exceptions, in the later Romantic concert repertoire. Grumiaux may perhaps be seen as a synthesis or mid-point between the playing styles of Oistrakh and Schneiderhan, virtuosic when called for but inward-turned as well. And a very important feature linking all three was their active participation as chamber musicians on a regular basis, each forming regular ties with colleagues which are well documented in both the official and live recording fields. I refer to the Oistrakh Trio, the Schneiderhan Quartet (and a Trio in which Schneiderhan worked with pianist Edwin Fischer and cellist Enrico Mainardi) and the Grumiaux Trio, the latter in particular often augmented to explore the field of the Classical String Quintet – in the discographies these participants are always named individually, as they were almost all established soloists in their own right.

In the case of David Oistrakh, a separate listing of his conducting work on record is added: although it is not uncommon for violinists to direct, say, the Mozart concerti from the violin, it is clear that in the later years of his career Oistrakh was thinking in terms of a future in which, like his colleague Yehudi Menuhin, he might no longer appear as a soloist but would weald the baton as a fully-fledged symphonic conductor.

For guidance with the discographies I have leaned heavily on The Disopaedia of the Violin 1889-1971 by James Creighton (University of Toronto Press 1974: a new edition was commenced in 1996 but appears not to have been completed); and in the case of Oistrakh on an internet listing by Paul Geffen. Many of Oistrakh's recordings having originated on the Melodiya label and been virtually unknown outside the USSR, it appears they were in many cases not even listed in the pioneering World's Encyclopedia of Recorded Music: numerous semi-official LP editions (Period, Monitor, Colosseum, Bruno) ensured their dissemination in the West. Russian Melodiya's logical but complex catalogue numbering system is explained in a Melodiya discography (Greenwood Press): suffice it here to state that each record side had its own number, thus the Beethoven Violin Sonatas appeared on S10 06363-06370 as a set of 4LPs (eight LP sides).

Designations for the main Moscow-based symphony orchestras often became somewhat blurred in translation, and I realise that I may have erred in the direction of over-simplification by sticking with the descriptions "USSR State Symphony" and "USSR (Large) Radio Orchestra".

My thanks to Michael Gray, Roderick Krüsemann, Alan Newcombe and Malcolm Walker for their usual additional assistance.

John Hunt 2004

Contents
David Oistrakh discography *page 7*
David Oistrakh as conductor *page 99*
Wolfgang Schneiderhan discography *page 109*
Arthur Grumiaux discography *page 147*

Great violinists

Caricatures from Im Konzertsaal karikiert (Langen-Müller 1960)

Great Violinists
Published by John Hunt.
© 2004 John Hunt
reprinted 2009
ISBN 978-1-901395-18-1

Sole distributors:
Travis & Emery,
17 Cecil Court,
London, WC2N 4EZ,
United Kingdom.
(+44) 20 7 459 2129.
sales@travis-and-emery.com

david oistrakh
1908-1974
the discography

ISAAC ALBENIZ (1860-1909)
love song from 6 italian songs, arranged for violin and piano by caterin

moscow 11 september 1940	topilin, piano	78: melodiya 10497-10489 lp: colosseum CRLP 105
moscow 1950	yampolsky, piano	lp: melodiya D 1201-1202/D 028807-028808 lp: colosseum CRLP 249 lp: bruno 14015 lp: eurodisc MK 86202 lp: monitor MC 2003 cd: monitor MCD 72003 cd: rca/bmg 74321 40710/74321 34180 cd: melodiya CD10 00745/CD10 00742

tango in d, arranged for violin and piano by dushkin

moscow 2 january 1934	topilin, piano	issued only in soviet russia *this recording was not listed in world's encyclopedia of recorded music*

ALFREDO D'AMBROSIO
serenata for violin and piano

moscow 20 january 1945	makarov, piano	78: melodiya 12458-12459

ARNO BABADZHANYAN (born 1921)
piano trio

moscow 1953	knushevitzky, cello babadzhanyan, piano	lp: melodiya D 1372-1373/M10 36363-36364 lp: colosseum CRLP 247 lp: monarch MWL 367 lp: chant du monde LDZA 8103

JOHANN SEBASTIAN BACH (1685-1750)
brandenburg concerto no 4

moscow 1959	moscow chamber orchestra barshai	lp: melodiya D 4432-4433/D 026219-026220 lp: monitor MC 2037 lp: parlophone PMB 1013
berlin ddr 19 april 1971	rundfunk- sinfonie-orchester waage	lp: melodiya M10 46419-46420

orchestral suite no 2

moscow 1959	moscow chamber orchestra barshai	lp: monitor MC 2037
moscow 1972	moscow philharmonic *oistrakh conducts from the violin*	lp: melodiya SM 03343-03344 lp: chant du monde LDX 78564 cd: zyx music ZYX 46114

violin concerto no 1 bwv 1041

moscow 1959	moscow chamber orchestra barshai	lp: melodiya D 5082-5083/D 08801-08802/ D 026 219-026 220 lp: artia ALP 165 lp: colosseum CRLP 254 lp: bruno 14008 lp: eurodisc XD 86243/XP 88665/KK 25931 lp: everest SDBR 3410 *also issued by marble classics, hispavox and recital hall*
london 1961	english chamber orchestra davis	dvd video: emi classic archive DVA 492 8369
vienna june 1962	vienna symphony *oistrakh conducts from the violin*	lp: dg LPM 18 820/SLPM 138 820/2535 109/ 2705 013/2721 180 cd: dg 419 8552/447 4272
berlin ddr 8 march 1965	rundfunk- sinfonie-orchester sanderling	lp: melodiya M10 46419-46420 cd: dante LYS 491-494
tokyo 18 april 1967	moscow philharmonic kondrashin	cd: altus (japan)

bach/**violin concerto no 2 bwv 1042**

berlin ddr	staatskapelle	cd: weitblick (japan) SSS 00192
17 september	konwitschny	*concert celebrating opening of the re-built*
1955		*deutsche staatsoper unter den linden*

philadelphia	philadelphia	lp: columbia (usa) ML 5087/MG 3328
24 december	orchestra	lp: philips ABL 3138/A01329L/G05650R
1955	ormandy	lp: eterna 825 612
		lp: melodiya M10 46429-46430
		lp: musidisc RC 818

moscow	moscow chamber	lp: melodiya D 08801-08802
1959	orchestra	lp: colosseum CRLP 254
	barshai	lp: bruno 14008
		lp: eurodisc XD 86243/XP 88665/XCK 80569
		lp: musidisc RC 856
		lp: everest SDBR 3410
		also issued by hispavox

vienna	vienna symphony	lp: dg LPM 18 820/SLPM 138 820/
june	*oistrakh conducts*	2535 109/2705 013
1962	*from the violin*	cd: dg 419 8552/447 4272

concerto for two violins bwv 1043

moscow	ussr state	cd: dante LYS 491-494
1946	symphony	cd: revelation RV 10066
	orlov	cd: doremi DHR 7760
	menuhin,	
	second violin	

leipzig	gewandhaus-	lp: dg LPE 17 160/LPM 18 393
april	orchester	lp: eterna 720 031
1957	konwitschny	lp: decca (usa) DL 9950
	i.oistrakh,	cd: berlin classics BC 21302/BC 02172
	second violin	

bucharest	bucharest	lp: melodiya M10 46361 006
18 september	philharmonic	
1958	georgescu	
	menuhin,	
	second violin	

bach/concerto for two violins bwv 1043/concluded

paris 24 october 1958	orchestre de chambre ortf capdevielle menuhin, second violin	dvd video: emi classic archive DVB 490 4499 *excerpt* vhs video: warner/nvc arts 8573 858013 dvd video: warner/nvc arts 8573 858012
moscow 1958	moscow chamber orchestra barshai i.oistrakh, second violin	lp: melodiya D 5082-5083/D 026219-026220 lp: bruno 14008 lp: eurodisc XD 86243/KK 25931 lp: monitor MC 2009 lp: hall of fame HOF 516/HOFS 516 lp: musidisc RC 856 lp: chant du monde LDX 8319 cd: chant du monde LDC 278906 cd: monitor MCD 72009 *also issued on cd by notablu*
london 26 february 1961	london philharmonic sargent i.oistrakh, second violin	unpublished radio broadcast *bbc london*
walthamstow february 1961	royal philharmonic goossens i.oistrakh, second violin	lp: dg LPM 18 714/LPM 18 820/135 082/ SLPM 138 714/SLPM 138 820/2535 176 lp: melodiya S 157-158/D 8267-8268 lp: eterna 720 162/826 030 lp: electrecord ECE 0889 cd: dg 419 8552/447 4272
moscow 19 march 1967	moscow philharmonic kondrashin i.oistrakh, second violin	cd: revelation RV 10039 cd: yedang classics CT 10031

bach/**concerto for violin and oboe bwv 1060**
vienna	vienna	lp: melodiya C10 25415-25416
8 june	philharmonic	
1972	sagftlain, oboe	
	oistrakh conducts	
	from the violin	

sonata in g for solo violin bwv 1001
date
uncertain
lp: melodiya D 04044-04045
cd: doremi DHR 7760
possibly also issued on lp by decca (usa)

sonata in c for two violins and keyboard bwv 1037
moscow	yampolsky, piano	lp: melodiya D 015349-015350/
1951	i.oistrakh,	D 004962-004963
	second violin	lp: bruno 14008
		lp: monitor MC 2005
		lp: chant du monde LDY 8138
		cd: monitor MCD 72005
		cd: doremi DHR 7760
		also issued on lp by colosseum and on 45 rpm by concert hall

leipzig	pischner,	lp: dg LPM 18 393
april	harpsichord	lp: dg heliodor 89 561
1957	i.oistrakh,	lp: eterna 720 037/820 283
	second violin	lp: decca (usa) DL 9950
		lp: heliodor (usa) H 25009/HS 25009
		cd: dg 463 6162

sonata for violin and keyboard bwv 1014
berlin ddr	pischner,	lp: dg LPEM 19 312/SLPEM 139 312/
october	harpsichord	2726 002/413 5151
1963		lp: eterna 825 798-825 799
		lp: melodiya C10 04763 003

sonata for violin and keyboard bwv 1015
berlin ddr	pischner,	lp: dg LPM 18 989/SLPM 138 989/
october	harpsichord	2726 002/413 5151
1963		lp: eterna 820 360/825 798-825 799
		lp: melodiya C10 04763 003

bach/**sonata for violin and keyboard   bwv 1016**
berlin ddr	pischner,	lp: dg LPM 18 989/SLPM 138 989/
october	harpsichord	2726 002/413 5151
1963		lp: eterna 820 360/825 798-825 799
		lp: melodiya C10 04763 003

sonata for violin and keyboard   bwv 1017
berlin ddr	pischner,	lp: dg LPEM 19 312/SLPEM 139 312/
october	harpsichord	2726 002/413 5151
1963		lp: eterna 825 798-825 799
		lp: melodiya C10 04763 003

sonata for violin and keyboard   bwv 1018
date	oborin, piano	lp: melodiya D 06335-06336
uncertain		lp: colosseum CRLP 193
		lp: chant du monde LDY 8108
		lp: kingsway KL 261
		lp: saga XID 5253
		lp: record hunter TRH 1
		also issued by bruno, eurodisc and monitor
berlin ddr	pischner,	lp: dg LPM 18 677/SLPM 138 677/
october	harpsichord	2726 002/413 5151
1963		lp: eterna 820 213/825 798-825 799
		lp: melodiya C10 04763 003

sonata for violin and keyboard   bwv 1019
moscow	yampolsky, piano	lp: melodiya D 03822-03823
1956		lp: bruno 14058
		lp: monitor MC 2009
		lp: monarch MWL 311
		also issued by chant du monde and decca (usa)
berlin ddr	pischner,	lp: dg LPM 18 677/SLPM 138 677/
october	harpsichord	2726 002/413 5151
1963		lp: eterna 820 213/825 798-825 799
		lp: melodiya C10 04763 003

BELA BARTOK (1881-1945)
violin concerto no 1

moscow 24 december 1960	ussr state symphony rozhdestvensky	cd: revelation RV 10015

moscow   ussr state   lp: melodiya S 0661-0662/D 010977-010978
25 august   symphony   lp: emi 1C063 63670
1962   rozhdestvensky lp: chant du monde LDXA 8333
                                                  lp: period SHO 342/SHOST 342
                                                  cd: jvc/melodiya (japan) VDC 1127
                                                  cd: chant du monde LDC 278941
                                                  cd: forlane UDC 16589
                                                  cd: urania (usa) US 5157

violin sonata no 1

prague   bauer, piano   cd: praga PR 250 038/PR 256 007
17 march
1972

moscow   richter, piano   lp: melodiya S10 05003-05004/
29 march-   S10 05441-05442
1 april   lp: emi ASD 3105/1C065 99150
1972   lp: columbia (usa) 36712
                                                  lp: eurodisc PK 89955
                                                  lp: chant du monde LDX 78673
                                                  cd: rca/bmg 74321 34182/74321 40710
                                                  cd: jvc/melodiya (japan) VDC 1114/VICC 2015
                                                  cd: melodiya CD10 00745/CD10 00744

salzburg   richter, piano   lp: rococo 2111
20 august
1972

bartok/**hungarian folksongs, arranged for violin and piano by szigeti**
moscow 1952	yampolsky, piano	lp: melodiya D 007529-007530/ D 028113-028114 lp: colosseum CRLP 249
prague 19 may 1969	bauer, piano	cd: praga PR 250 038/PR 256 007

rumanian folkdances, arranged for violin and piano by szekely
moscow 13 march 1947	kollegorskaya, piano	78: melodiya 14653-14654
moscow 1952	yampolsky, piano	lp: supraphon LPM 257/SVEC 807/ MKS 25007 lp: parliament PLP 118 lp: colosseum CRLP 249

LUDWIG VAN BEETHOVEN (1770-1827)
violin concerto

moscow 1950-1951	ussr large radio orchestra gauk	78: melodiya 019230-019241 lp: melodiya D 0498-0499 lp: bruno 14020 lp: colosseum CRLP 155 lp: eurodisc XPK 88665 lp: concert hall CHS 1303/MMS 2017 lp: fidelio ATL 4022 lp: musidisc RC 610 lp: period SHO 316/SPL 598 lp: vox STPL 516150 lp: whitehall 335013 cd: dante LYS 331-334 cd: rca/bmg GD 69055 *also issued by other labels including joker, allegro and everest*
berlin ddr 31 march 1952	rundfunk- sinfonie-orchester abendroth	lp: melodiya M10 46341 002 cd: arlecchino ARL 164 cd: melodram MEL 18020 cd: bella musica 31.6003/CD 962 cd: pilz 78000 cd: scribendum SC 009 cd: tahra TAH 129-131 *melodram and arlecchino versions incorrecty dated 1950; also unpublished video footage filmed at rehearsals*

beethoven/violin concerto/concluded

stockholm 10-11 june 1954	stockholm festival orchestra ehrling	lp: columbia 33CX 1194 lp: columbia (france) FCX 354/FCX 30077 lp: columbia (italy) QCX 10120 lp: columbia (germany) WCX 1194/C 90386 lp: hmv (spain) LALP 231 lp: angel 35162 cd: testament SBT 1032

paris
8-10
november
1958
	orchestre national
	cluytens
		lp: columbia 33CX 1672/SAX 2315
		lp: columbia (france) FCX 817/SAXF 119
		lp: columbia (italy) QCX 10384/SAXQ 7275
		lp: columbia (germany) WCX 1672/SAXW 2315/
		    C 91051/STC 91051
		lp: angel 35780/34457
		lp: melodiya D 033639-033640
		lp: emi SLS 5004/XLP 30168/SXLP 30168/
		    SHZE 143/1C037 90905/1C065 90905
		cd: emi CDM 769 2612/483 4182
		cd: notablu 93.5107

milan 1960	rai milano orchestra gui	lp: cetra LAR 3 cd: cetra CDAR 2028 cd: arkadia CDMP 4181/CD 34018
lisbon 27 june 1960	national orchestra of portugal freitas branco	cd: portugalsom SP 4078
berlin ddr 14 october 1960	staatskapelle konwitschny	cd: weitblick (japan) SSS 00192
naples 15 april 1965	rai napoli orchestra albert	cd: melodram CDM 28034
london 10 october 1965	moscow philharmonic kondrashin	cd: bbc legends BBCL 41272
vienna 25 may 1974	vienna symphony giulini	cd: live classics best (japan) LCB 106 *orchestra incorrectly described as vienna philharmonic*

version of the beethoven concerto on everest SDBR 3343 attributed to oistrakh but probably contains a performance by leonid kogan

beethoven/**triple concerto**

moscow 1947	ussr large radio orchestra golovanov oborin, piano knushevitsky, cello	lp: melodiya D 026327-026328 lp: colosseum CRLP 10200 lp: period SHO 327/SPL 590 lp: musidisc RC 824 lp: eurodisc ZK 80533 lp: bruno 14039 cd: dante LYS 491-494 cd: doremi DHR 7714 *some editions incorrectly name conductor as orlov*

london
10 may
1958
	philharmonia
	sargent
	oborin, piano
	knushevitsky,
	cello
		lp: columbia 33C 1062/SBO 2753
		lp: columbia (italy) QCX 10351/SAXQ 7312
		lp: columbia (germany) WC 525/SBOW 2753/
		    C 70387/STC 70387
		lp: angel 35697/36727/34400
		lp: melodiya D 22551-22552
		lp: emi XLP 20081/SXLP 20081/SXLP 30378/
		    SHZE 706/SREG 1098/1C037 01974/
		    1C053 01974
		cd: emi CDZ 762 8542/CDM 769 3312/
		    CDFB 69331/483 4182/826 6542

moscow 1961	ussr state symphony ivanov oborin, piano knushevitsky, cello	cd: multisonic 31.0104

berlin brd
15-17
september
1969
	berlin
	philharmonic
	karajan
	richter, piano
	rostropovich,
	cello
		lp: emi ASD 2582/1C065 02042/2C069 02042/
		    3C065 02042
		lp: angel 36727
		lp: melodiya CM 02021-02022
		lp: supraphon SV 11 00898
		lp: eterna 826 226
		cd: emi CDM 769 0322/CDM 764 7442/
		    CDM 566 0922/CMS 566 1122/CDM 566 2192/
		    566 9022
		third movement
		cd: emi HVKBPO 1

moscow 5 january 1970	moscow philharmonic kondrashin richter, piano rostropovich, cello	vhs video: emi MVD 491 3013 laserdisc: emi LDB 491 3011 *excerpts* cd: emi CZS 572 0162 vhs video: warner/nvc arts 3984 230293

beethoven/**violin romance no 1**

moscow 15 march 1948	ussr state symphony kondrashin	lp: melodiya D 001224-001225 cd: revelation RV 10015 cd: doremi DHR 7714 cd: urania URN 22233
berlin ddr 31 march 1952	rundfunk- sinfonie-orchester abendroth	cd: melodram MEL 18020 cd: bella musica 31.6003 cd: tahra TAH 129-131 cd: scribendum SC 009 *melodram incorrectly dated 1950; tahra incorrectly dated 23 november 1952*
berlin ddr 7 april 1952	yampolsky, piano	lp: melodiya M10 463461 002
walthamstow february 1961	royal philharmonic goossens	45: dg EPL 30 586/SEPL 121 586 lp: dg LPM 18 714/SLPM 138 714/ 135 039/2720 008 lp: melodiya D 08285-08286/SM 0155-0156 cd: dg 413 8442/447 4272
berlin ddr 8 march 1965	rundfunk- sinfonie-orchester sanderling	lp: melodiya M10 46419 002 cd: dante LYS 491-494
moscow 12 november 1966	ussr state symphony rozhdestvensky	dvd video: emi classic archive DVB 599 6859
moscow 27 september 1968	moscow philharmonic rozhdestvensky	cd: rca/bmg 74321 729142

beethoven/**violin romance no 2**

moscow 1947	ussr state symphony kondrashin	lp: melodiya D 07587-07588/ D 026327-026328 cd: dante LYS 491-494 cd: rca/bmg GD 69055 cd: doremi DHR 7714 cd: urania URN 22233
berlin ddr 31 march 1952	rundfunk- sinfonie-orchester abendroth	unpublished radio broadcast *ddr rundfunk tapes apparently mislaid*
prague 27 april 1954	czech philharmonic ancerl	lp: supraphon LPV 244/SUA 10127/11 0582 lp: eterna 820 565 cd: supraphon SU 3005/SU 1936.2011/ 3685 2001
berlin ddr 17 september 1955	staatskapelle konwitschny	cd: weitblick (japan) SSS 00192 *concert celebrating opening of the re-built* *deutsche staatsoper unter den linden*
date uncertain	moscow chamber orchestra barshai	lp: vanguard VCS 4020 lp: period SHO 343/SHOST 343 lp: hall of fame HOF 519/HOFS 519 *also issued by melodiya and bruno*
walthamstow february 1961	royal philharmonic goossens	45: dg EPL 30 586/SEPL 121 586 lp: dg LPM 18 714/SLPM 138 714/ 135 039/2720 008 lp: melodiya D 08285-08286/SM 0155-0156 cd: dg 413 8442/447 4272
moscow 27 september 1968	moscow philharmonic rozhdestvensky	cd: rca/bmg 74321 729142

beethoven/**minuet in g, arranged for violin and piano by kreisler**
moscow   topilin, piano   78: melodiya 7591-7592
31 october   *this recording was not listed in world's encyclopedia*
1938   *of recorded music*

string quartet no 10 "the harp"
date   bondarenko,   78: melodiya 021241-021250
uncertain   violin   lp: melodiya D 1308-1309/D 07597-07598
                       terian, viola   cd: doremi DHR 7750
                       knushevitsky,   *possibly also issued by eurodisc*
                       cello

trio op 25 for flute, violin and viola
date   madetov, flute   lp: melodiya D 7549-7550
uncertain   terian, viola   *this recording was not listed in world's encyclopedia*
                                                      of recorded music

violin sonata op 12 no 1
prague   yampolsky, piano   lp: supraphon LPV 244/SUA 10127
1954   lp: eterna 820 565
                                                     cd: supraphon 11.0582

paris   oborin, piano   lp: philips AL 3416/SAL 3416/A02269L/
18 may-   835 245AY/6768 036
19 june   lp: philips (usa) PHM 500 032/PHS 900 032
1962   lp: melodiya D 010763-010764/S 0477-0478/
                                                     S10 06363-06370
                                                    lp: eterna 825 951
                                                    lp: chant du monde LDXA 8301
                                                    cd: philips 412 5702

paris   oborin, piano   lp: cetra DOC 57
16 june   cd: doremi DHR 7807-7809
1962

a filmed fragment from this sonata with oistrakh and the pianist sviatoslav richter appears on warner/ nvc arts 3984 230303 (vhs video) and 3984 230302 (dvd video)

beethoven/**violin sonata op 12 no 2**

paris
18 may-
19 june
1962
	oborin, piano	lp: philips AL 3417/SAL 3417/A02770L/
		    835 245AY/6768 036
		lp: philips (usa) PHM 500 033/PHS 900 033
		lp: melodiya D 010763-010764/S 0477-0478/
		    S10 06363-06370
		lp: eterna 826 952
		lp: chant du monde LDXA 8301
		cd: philips 412 5702

paris 15 june 1962	oborin, piano	lp: cetra DOC 57 cd: doremi DHR 7807-7809

violin sonata op 12 no 3

brussels 19 may 1955	yampolsky, piano	lp: columbia 33CX 1580 lp: columbia (italy) QCX 10324 lp: columbia (france) FCX 581 lp: hmv (spain) LALP 365 lp: angel 35331 cd: testament SBT 1115 *possibly also issued on the colosseum label*

paris
18 may-
19 june
1962
	oborin, piano	lp: philips AL 3418/SAL 3418/A02271L/
		    835 152AY/6768 036/6558 009
		lp: philips (usa) PHM 500 033/PHS 900 033
		lp: melodiya D 010763-010764/S 0479-0480/
		    S10 06363-06370
		lp: eterna 826 951
		lp: chant du monde LDXA 8301
		cd: philips 412 5702

paris 19 june 1962	oborin, piano	lp: cetra DOC 57 cd: doremi DHR 7807-7809
moscow 6-7 may 1970	richter, piano	laserdisc: emi LDB 491 3011 vhs video: emi MVD 491 3013

beethoven/**violin sonata op 23**

moscow 1950	goldenweiser, piano	lp: melodiya D 07893-07894 *this recording was not listed in world's encyclopedia of recorded music*

paris
18 may-
19 june
1962
	oborin, piano	lp: philips AL 3418/SAL 3418/A02271L/
		    835 152AY/6768 036
		lp: philips (usa) PHM 500 033/PHS 900 033
		lp: melodiya D 010765-010766/S 0479-0480/
		    S10 06363-06370
		lp: eterna 826 952
		lp: chant du monde LDXA 8302
		cd: philips 412 5702

paris 15 june 1962	oborin, piano	lp: cetra DOC 57 cd: doremi DHR 7807-7809

violin sonata op 24 "spring"

moscow 1950	oborin, piano	78: melodiya 18882-18889 lp: melodiya D 1296-1297/D 07893-07894 lp: colosseum CRLP 152 lp: period SPL 573 lp: chant du monde LDZA 8110 *period incorrectly names accompanist as yampolsky*

paris
18 may-
19 june
1962
	oborin, piano	lp: philips AL 3420/SAL 3420/A02273L/
		    835 154AY/6768 036/6570 058
		lp: philips (usa) PHM 500 030/PHS 900 030
		lp: melodiya D 010767-010768/S 0481-0482/
		    S10 06363-06370
		lp: eterna 826 952
		lp: chant du monde LDXA 8303
		cd: philips 412 5702/412 2552

paris 18may 1962	oborin, piano	lp: cetra DOC 57 cd: doremi DHR 7807-7809 dvd video: emi classic archive DVA 492 8369 *emi classic archive dated 7 june 1962*
prague 19 may 1969	bauer, piano	cd: praga PR 250 058/PR 256 007

beethoven/**violin sonata op 30 no 1**

paris
18 may-
19 june
1962
	oborin, piano	lp: philips AL 3420/SAL 3420/A02273L/
		     835 154AY/6768 036
		lp: philips (usa) PHM 500 032/PHS 900 032
		lp: melodiya D 010767-010768/S 0481-0482/
		     D 011255-011258
		lp: eterna 826 953
		lp: chant du monde LDXA 8303
		cd: philips 412 5702

paris 19 june 1962	oborin, piano	lp: cetra DOC 57 cd: doremi DHR 7807-7809
paris 4 december 1968	richter, piano	cd: chant du monde LDC 278885 *adagio movement only*

violin sonata op 30 no 2

moscow 1949	oborin, piano	lp: melodiya D 07637-07638
paris 18 may- 19 june 1962	oborin, piano	lp: philips AL 3418/SAL 3418/A02227L/ 835 152AY/6768 036 lp: philips (usa) PHM 500 030/PHS 900 030 lp: melodiya D 010765-010766/S 0483-0484 lp: eterna 826 954 lp: chant du monde LDXA 8303 cd: philips 412 5702
paris 18 may 1962	oborin, piano	lp: cetra DOC 57 cd: doremi DHR 7807-7809

violin sonata op 30 no 3

moscow 1950	oborin, piano	lp: melodiya D 07637-07638/D 017293-017296
moscow 4 june 1960	oborin, piano	cd: living masters LM 1330 cd: icone 9403
paris 18 may- 19 june 1962	oborin, piano	lp: philips AL 3416/SAL 3416/A02269L/ 835 150AY/6768 036 lp: philips (usa) PHM 500 033/PHS 900 033 lp: melodiya D 010769-010770/S 0483-0484 lp: eterna 826 951 lp: chant du monde LDXA 8304 cd: philips 412 5702
paris 15 june 1962	oborin, piano	lp: cetra DOC 57 cd: doremi DHR 7807-7809

beethoven/**violin sonata op 47 "kreutzer"**

paris june 1953	oborin, piano	lp: columbia 33C 1047 lp: columbia (germany) WC 1047/C 70100 lp: hmv (spain) LBLP 1050 lp: melodiya D 03894-03895 lp: colosseum CRLP 153 lp: monitor MC 2042 lp: musical appreciation society 572 lp: chant du monde LDA 8077 lp: vanguard VRS 6024 cd: vanguard OVC 4080-4082 cd: testament SBT 1115
paris 18 may- 19 june 1962	oborin, piano	lp: philips AL 3419/SAL 3419/A02272L/ 835 153AY/6768 036/6558 009 lp: philips (usa) PHM 500 031/PHS 900 031 lp: melodiya D 010771-010772/S 0485-0486 lp: eterna 826 953 lp: chant du monde LDXA 8304 cd: philips 412 5702/412 2552
paris 19 june 1962	oborin, piano	lp: cetra DOC 57 cd: doremi DHR 7807-7809
tokyo 1967	bauer, piano	lp: rococo 2097 *rehearsal extract* vhs video: warner/nvc arts 3984 230303 dvd video: warner/nvc arts 3984 230302 dvd video: emi classic archive SVB 599 6859

violin sonata op 96

moscow 1956	oborin, piano	lp: monitor MC 2042
paris 18 may- 19 june 1962	oborin, piano	lp: philips AL 3417/SAL 3417/A02270L/ 835 151AY/6768 036 lp: philips (usa) PHM 6500 031/PHS 900 031 lp: melodiya D 010769-010770/S 0487-0488 lp: eterna 826 954 lp: chant du monde LDXA 8304 cd: philips 412 5702
paris 15 june 1962	oborin, piano	lp: cetra DOC 57 cd: doremi DHR 7807-7809

beethoven/**piano trio no 3**
date	oborin, piano	lp: melodiya D 015359-015360/
uncertain	knushevitsky,	M10 48855-48856
	cello	*also issued in japan by jvc; recording not listed in world's encyclopedia of recorded music*

piano trio no 4 "ghost"
date	oborin, piano	lp: melodiya D 015359-015360/
uncertain	knushevitsky,	M10 48855-48856
	cello	*also issued in japan by jvc; recording not listed in world's encyclopedia of recorded music*

piano trio no 6 "archduke"
london	oborin, piano	lp: columbia 33CX 1643/SAX 2352
9-12	knushevitsky,	lp: columbia (france) FCX 30526/SAXF 130526
may	cello	lp: columbia (italy) QCX 10377/SAXQ 7300
1958		lp: columbia (germany) WSX 552/C 80542/ SCXW 7518/STC 80542/SMC 80542
		lp: angel 35704
		lp: melodiya S10 5735-5736
		lp: emi MFP 2117/1C047 00866/2C037 01974
		cd: emi CZS 569 3672

JIRI BENDA (1722-1795)
trio sonata in e for two violins and keyboard
leipzig	yampolsky, piano	45: dg EPL 30 294
april	i.oistrakh,	lp: dg LP 16 136
1957	second violin	lp: dg heliodor 89 561/478 132
		lp: eterna 720 037/820 283
		lp: decca (usa) DL 9962
		lp: heliodor (usa) H 25009/HS 25009
		cd: dg 463 6162

26
JOHANNES BRAHMS (1833-1897)
violin concerto

moscow 1952	ussr large radio orchestra kondrashin	78: melodiya D 021869-021877 lp: melodiya D 0857-0858/D 07387-07388 lp: colosseum CRLP 150 lp: bruno 14004 lp: hall of fame HOF 508/HOFS 508 lp: period SHO 336/SHOST 336 lp: monarch MWL 310 lp: musidisc RC 853 lp: vanguard VRS 6018 lp: chant du monde LDA 8106 lp: vox VSPS 3 lp: murray hall S-2760 lp: telefunken BLE 14019 lp: saga XID 5231 lp: eurodisc 200.452 200/KK 73606 lp: westminster WGM 8260 cd: supraphon SUCD 10 00212 cd: dante LYS 491-494 cd: vanguard OCD 1024 cd: chant du monde LDC 278 942 cd: rca/bmg 74321 341792/74321 407102 cd: melodiya CD10 00745/CD10 00741 cd: urania URN 22233 *eurodisc and westminster editions incorrectly name conductor as igor oistrakh*
berlin ddr 31 march 1952	rundfunk- sinfonie-orchester abendroth	cd: tahra TAH 145-146
berlin ddr 16 february 1954	dresden staatskapelle konwitschny	lp: dg LPM 18 199/2726 087 lp: dg heliodor 89 607/478 137 lp: eterna LPM 1015/820 003 lp: supraphon DV 5411 lp: decca (usa) DL 9754/DXB 141 lp: heliodor (usa) H 25091/HS 25091 cd: dg 423 3992/447 4272/459 0162
berlin ddr 17 september 1955	staatskapelle konwitschny	cd: weitblick (japan) SSS 00192 *concert celebrating opening of the re-built deutsche staatsoper unter den linden*

brahms/violin concerto/continued

london 11 may 1958	bbc symphony schwarz	unpublished video recording for bbc television *third movement* dvd video: emi classic archive DVA 492 8369

paris
17-19
june
1960
	orchestre
	national
	klemperer
		lp: columbia 33CX 1765/SAX 2411
		lp: columbia (france) FCX 879/SAXF 196
		lp: columbia (italy) QCX 10477/SAXQ 7347
		lp: columbia (germany) WCX 560/C 91134/
		    SAXW 9542/STC 91134
		lp: angel 35836/32031
		lp: emi SLS 5004/CFP 4398/SXLP 30264/
		    1C037 00534/2C181 52289-52290/
		    1C053 00534/2C059 00534/
		    1C177 05777-05781
		cd: emi CDM 764 6232/CDM 769 0342/
		    CZS 479 8902/574 5592/574 7242

london 26 february 1961	london philharmonic sargent	cd: bbc legends BBCL 41022
prague 31 may 1961	czech philharmonic pedrotti	cd: multisonic 31.0020 cd: supraphon SU 37802
lugano 11 june 1961	swiss-italian radio orchestra nussio	cd: ermitage ERM 162
leningrad 1961	leningrad philharmonic rozhdestvensky	cd: leningrad masters LM 1330 cd: icone 9403
moscow 8 february 1963	moscow philharmonic kondrashin	cd: rca/bmg 74321 729142 cd: revelation RV 10015
moscow 14 february 1966	moscow philharmonic rozhdestvensky	dvd video: emi classic archive DVB 599 6859 *excerpt* vhs video: warner/nvc arts 3984 230301 dvd video: warner/nvc arts 3984 230302
tokyo 16 april 1967	moscow philharmonic rozhdestvensky	cd: altus (japan)

28
brahms/violin concerto/concluded

paris 30 may 1967	orchestre national bruck	cd: ina mémoire vive 262007
date uncertain	munich philharmonic rieger	cd: topazio (japan) 26048

cleveland
19 may
1969
	cleveland
	orchestra
	szell
		lp: emi SLS 786/ASD 2525/2C069 02008/
		    3C065 02008
		lp: angel 36033/32096/34412
		lp: eurodisc MK 80184/XFK 27945/
		    XGK 86095/XPK 88665
		lp: melodiya SM 01861-01862
		lp: supraphon 11 1042 21-25
		cd: emi 567 9732

vienna 11 june 1972	vienna philharmonic abbado	lp: melodiya C10 25145-25146

double concerto

leningrad 1948	leningrad radio orchestra eliasberg knushevitsky, cello	lp: melodiya D 4848-4849 lp: monarch MWL 333 lp: period SHO 336/SHOST 336 lp: ricordi OCL 16263 lp: vibraton VBK 2037 lp: vox PL 16390 cd: chant du monde LDC 278942 cd: dante LYS 354 *period and vibraton editions incorrectly name* *conductor as kondrashin*
prague 1949	prague radio orchestra ancerl sadlo, cello	78: supraphon G 23282-23285 78: ultraphon G 15430-15433 78: eurochord TA 1738-1741 lp: supraphon 010 2372 lp: eurodisc 300.267 420 lp: bruno 14039 lp: colosseum CRLP 120 lp: classic edition SR 8 cd: dante LYS 353 *world's encyclopedia of recorded music suggested that* *orchestra was czech philharmonic*

brahms/double concerto/concluded

london
29 february-
3 march
1956
	philharmonia
	galliera
	fournier, cello
		lp: columbia 33CX 1487/SAX 2264
		lp: columbia (italy) QCX 10378/SAXQ 7264
		lp: columbia (france) FC 1048/SAXF 143
		lp: columbia (germany) WC 520/C 70383/
		    SBOW 8501/STC 70383
		lp: hmv (spain) LALP 498
		lp: angel 35353
		lp: emi XLP 30185/SXLP 30185/EMX 2035/
		    SHZE 706/1C037 01974/2C069 01974/
		    2C181 52289-52290
		cd: emi CDZ 762 8542/CZS 569 3312/
		    CDFB 69331/826 6592

london september 1965	moscow philharmonic kondrashin rostropovich, cello	dvd video: emi classic archive DVA 490 4499

cleveland
12-13
may
1969
	cleveland
	orchestra
	szell
	rostropovich,
	cello
		lp: emi SLS 786/ASD 3312/1C065 02009/
		    2C069 02009/3C065 02009
		lp: angel 35032/34400
		lp: melodiya SM 01861-01862
		lp: eterna 826 322
		lp: chant du monde LDX 78495
		cd: emi CDM 764 7442/CMS 565 7012/
		    CDM 566 9022/253 6582

stockholm 9 september 1971	swedish radio orchestra westerberg olofsson, cello	lp: bis BISLP 331-333

violin sonata no 1

moscow 5 january 1957	oborin, piano	cd: revelation RV 10016
vienna may 1970	bauer, piano	lp: melodiya SM 02931-02932 lp: angel 40197 lp: musical heritage society MHS 4551 lp: eurodisc 300.609 420 lp: ricordi OCL 16231 *also issued by hispavox and jvc*
prague 17 june 1972	bauer, piano	cd: praga PR 250 058/PR 256 007

brahms/**violin sonata no 2**

moscow	richter, piano	lp: melodiya C10 05003-05004/
19 march		C10 05003 007
1972		lp: emi ASD 3425/1C063 97791/2C065 97791/
		3C065 97791
		lp: angel 40268
		lp: eurodisc MK 87954/XRK 27315/
		300.609 420
		lp: chant du monde C 5003
		lp: musical heritage society MHS 4577
		lp: supraphon 111 2175
		cd: chant du monde LDC 278881
		cd: zyx melodiya 46038
		cd: rca/bmg 74321 341802/74321 407102
		cd: melodiya CD10 00745/CD10 00743
salzburg	richter, piano	lp: rococo 2111
20 august		cd: orfeo C498 981B
1972		*also issued on cd by deagostini*

brahms/**violin sonata no 3**

berlin ddr 7 april 1952	yampolsky, piano	78: ultraphon E 22324-22326 lp: melodiya M10 46361-46362 lp: colosseum CRLP 148 *also issued by victor in japan*
brussels 19 may 1955	yampolsky, piano	lp: columbia 33CX 1580 lp: columbia (italy) QCX 10324 lp: columbia (france) FCX 581/FCX 30269 lp: hmv (spain) LALP 365 lp: angel 35331
prague 18 may 1966	bauer, piano	cd: praga PR 250 058/PR 256 007
paris 4 december 1968	richter, piano	lp: chant du monde LDX 78444 cd: chant du monde LDC 278881

moscow
28 december
1968
	richter, piano	lp: emi ASD 2618/1C063 99240/
		  2C065 99240/3C065 99240
		lp: melodiya D 025827-025828/
		  CM 02257-02258/C10 02257 000
		lp: angel 40121
		lp: eurodisc KK 80080/XRK 27315/
		  300.609 420
		lp: eterna 826 214
		lp: musical heritage society MHS 3956
		lp: quintessence PMC 7133
		cd: rca/bmg 74321 341812/74321 407102
		cd: melodiya CD10 00745/CD10 00743

new york 1-4 february 1970	richter, piano	vhs video: warner/nvc arts 3984 230293 dvd video: warner/nvc arts 3984 230292 *short excerpt only*

brahms/**scherzo in c minor/fae sonata**

moscow 13 october 1945	yampolsky, piano	lp: melodiya D 13249-13250 lp: colosseum CRLP 105
paris 29 march 1962	bauer, piano	dvd video: emi classic archive DVA 492 8369
paris 4 december 1968	richter, piano	cd: chant du monde LDC 278881

string quartet op 51 no 1

date uncertain	bondarenko, violin terian, viola knushevitsky, cello	lp: melodiya D 07281-07282 cd: doremi DHR 7750

clarinet quintet

date uncertain	sorokin, clarinet bondarenko, violin terian, viola knushevitsky, cello	lp: melodiya D 03074-03075 lp: bruno 14062 cd: doremi DHR 7702

wiegenlied, arranged for violin and piano

moscow 1956	oborin, piano	lp: monitor MC 2003/MC 2042 lp: hall of fame HOF 519/HOFS 519 cd: monitor MCD 72003

hungarian dance no 5, arranged for violin and piano by joachim

moscow 14 august 1947	kollegorskaya, piano	78: melodiya 15058-15059

moscow 1952	yampolsky, piano	lp: melodiya D 1201-1202/D 029743-029744 lp: supraphon DM 5166 lp: ultraphon C 5166 lp: bruno 14004 lp: colosseum CRLP 149 lp: monarch MWL 333 lp: vanguard VRS 6020 cd: rca/bmg 74321 341802/74321 470102 cd: vanguard OVC 4080-4082 cd: melodiya C10 00745/CD10 00742

hungarian dance no 7, arranged for violin and piano by joachim

berlin ddr 7 april 1952	yampolsky, piano	lp: melodiya M10 46361-46362

hungarian dance no 8, arranged for violin and piano by joachim

moscow 14 august 1947	kollegorskaya, piano	78: melodiya 15058-15059

moscow 1952	yampolsky, piano	lp: melodiya D 1201-1202/D 029743-029744 lp: supraphon DM 5166 lp: ultraphon C 5166 lp: bruno 14004 lp: colosseum CRLP 149 lp: monarch MWL 333 lp: vanguard VRS 6020 cd: rca/bmg 74321 341802/74321 470102 cd: vanguard OVC 4080-4082 cd: melodiya CD10 00745/CD10 00742

hungarian dance no 9, arranged for violin and piano by joachim

moscow 1952	yampolsky, piano	lp: melodiya D 1201-1202/D 22332-22333 lp: supraphon DM 5166 lp: ultraphon C 5166 lp: bruno 14004 lp: colosseum CRLP 149 lp: vanguard VRS 6020 cd: rca/bmg 74321 341802/74321 470102 cd: vanguard OVC 4080-4082 cd: melodiya CD10 00745/CD10 00742

hungarian dance no 11, arranged for violin and piano by joachim

moscow 1952	yampolsky, piano	lp: melodiya D 22332-22333

brahms/**hungarian dance no 20, arranged for violin and piano by joachim**

moscow 14 august 1947	kollegorskaya, piano	78: melodiya 15058-15059

moscow 1952	yampolsky, piano	lp: melodiya D 1201-1202/D 10462-10463 lp: supraphon LPM 184 lp: monitor MC 2003 lp: hall of fame HOF 519/HOFS 519 cd: monitor MCD 72003 cd: rca/bmg 74321 341802/74321 470102 cd: melodiya CD10 00745/CD10 00742 *hall of fame edition describes pianist as oborin*

MAX BRUCH (1838-1920)
violin concerto no 1

date uncertain	ussr state symphony gauk	lp: melodiya lp: colosseum CRLP 225 lp: bruno 14003 cd: dante LYS 353 *this recording was not listed in world's encyclopedia* *of recorded music*

london
17-18
november
1954
	london
	symphony
	matacic
		lp: columbia 33CX 1268
		lp: columbia (france) FCX 419/FCX 30245/
		    FC 25119
		lp: columbia (germany) WCX 1268/C 90438/
		    WS 523/C 60548
		lp: columbia (italy) QCX 10248
		lp: hmv (spain) LALP 255
		lp: angel 35243
		lp: melodiya D 021421-021422
		lp: emi SLS 5003/XLP 30109/SMVP 8028/
		    HC 126/1C047 50510
		cd: emi CDM 769 2612

scottish fantasy for violin and orchestra

moscow 24 december 1960	ussr state symphony rozhdestvensky	cd: revelation RV 10051

london 13-14 september 1962	london symphony horenstein	lp: decca LXT 6035/SXL 6035/SDD 465 lp: decca (germany) 642 514AH lp: london (usa) CM 9337/CS 9337 cd: decca 470 2582

GEORGI LVOVICH CATOIRE (1861-1926)
elegy for violin and piano
moscow	goldenweiser,	78: melodiya 1408-1409
1951	piano	cd: doremi DHR 7720

violin sonata no 1
moscow	goldenweiser,	lp: melodiya D 026217-026218
1952	piano	cd: doremi DHR 7720

violin sonata no 2
moscow	goldenweiser,	lp: melodiya D 026217-026218/M10 37533 000
1948	piano	cd: doremi DHR 7720
		cd: dante HPC 103

ERNEST CHAUSSON (1855-1899)
poeme pour violon et orchestre
moscow	ussr state	lp: melodiya D 03040-03041
15 march	symphony	lp: bruno 14009
1948	kondrashin	lp: colosseum CRLP 253
		lp: monitor MC 2073
		lp: eurodisc XPK 88665/XK 80569
		lp: chant du monde LDM 8173/LDX 8359
		lp: napoleon NLC 16034
		lp: westminster XWN 18177/WGM 8251
		cd: monitor MCD 72073
		cd: melodiya SUCD 10 00219
		cd: chant du monde LDC 278908
		cd: dante LYS 355
		cd: revelation RV 10015

boston	boston	lp: victor LM 1988/RB 16166/VIC 1058/
14 december	symphony	VICS 1058/GM 43367
1955	munch	lp: hmv ALP 1460
		lp: melodiya D 021421-021422
		cd: rca/bmg GD 60683

FREDERIC CHOPIN (1810-1849)
piano trio in g
moscow	oborin, piano	lp: melodiya D 4882-4883
1950	knushevitsky,	lp: bruno 14012
	cello	lp: colosseum CRLP 251
		lp: monitor MC 2069
		lp: westminster XWN 18174
		cd: monitor MCD 72069

chopin/étude op 25 no 2, arranged for violin and piano by burmeister
moscow   topilin, piano   issued only in soviet russia
1932

mazurka op 33 no 2, arranged for violin and piano by kreisler
warsaw   topilin, piano   78: syrena 8602
1935   78: bellacord 3828

mazurka op 67 no 4, arranged for violin and piano by kreisler
moscow   topilin, piano   issued only in soviet russia
1932

1937-1939   makarov, piano   78: melodiya 5520-5521

nocturne op 9 no 2, arranged for violin and piano by sarasate
moscow   makarov, piano   78: melodiya 12456-12457
20 january   78: chant du monde GA 5002
1945   78: mercury DM 27
                                   78: supraphon G 22207
                                   78: ultraphon G 14742
                                   45: mercury EP 15008
                                   lp: mercury MG 10035
                                   lp: colosseum CRLP 110

nocturne op 72 no 1, arranged for violin and piano by auer
moscow   yampolsky, piano   78: melodiya 017369-017370
27 october
1949

nocturne in c sharp minor op posth, arranged for violin and piano by rodionov
moscow   yampolsky, piano   78: melodiya 017369-017370
27 october
1949

berlin ddr   yampolsky, piano   lp: melodiya M10 46361 002
7 april
1952

valse op 64 no 2, arranged for violin and piano by huberman
warsaw   topilin, piano   78: syrena 8602
1935   78: bellacord 3828

with the exception of nocturne op 9 no 2 these chopin transciptions were not listed in world's encyclopedia of recorded music

LOUIS DAQUIN (1694-1772)
le coucou, arranged for violin and piano by manen
moscow	makarov, piano	78: melodiya 5520-5521
10 august		*this recording was not listed in world's encyclopedia*
1937		*of recorded music*

CLAUDE DEBUSSY (1862-1918)
violin sonata in g
paris	bauer, piano	lp: philips SAL 3589/802 727AY/6570 206
2 february		lp: philips (usa) PHM 500 112/PHS 900 112
1966		lp: melodiya D 020403-020404/
		S 01527-01528
		lp: chant du monde LDX 78712
		cd: chant du monde LDC 278944
		cd: philips 420 7772

beau soir, arranged for violin and piano by heifetz
moscow	makarov, piano	cd: rca/bmg 74321 407102/74321 341802
1946		cd: melodiya CD10 00745/CD10 00742

clair de lune, arranged for violin and piano by roelens
london	yampolsky, piano	45: columbia SEL 1577/ESL 6252/SEB 2515
28 february		45: columbia (italy) SEBQ 219/ESLQ 1007
1956		lp: columbia 33CX 1466/SAX 2253
		lp: columbia (france) SAXF 149
		lp: columbia (germany) WSX 604/SHZE 160
		lp: angel 35354/60259
		cd: testament SBT 1116
		cd: emi 562 9142
		also issued by melodiya, eterna, bruno and jvc

paris	bauer, piano	dvd video: emi classic archive DVA 492 6389
27 march		
1962		

passepied/suite bergamasque, arranged for violin and piano by caramba
moscow	makarov, piano	cd: rca/bmg 74321 407102/74321 341802
1946		cd: melodiya CD10 00745/CD10 00742
		this recording was not listed in world's encyclopedia
		of recorded music

la plus que lente, arranged for violin and piano
moscow	unnamed pianist	vhs video: warner/nvc arts 3984 230303
1936		dvd video: warner/nvc arts 3984 230302

ANTONIN DVORAK (1841-1904)
violin concerto

moscow	ussr state	lp: melodiya D 03064-03065
1949	symphony	lp: mk records DO 3064
	kondrashin	lp: bruno 14021
		lp: colosseum CRLP 137
		lp: musidisc RC 868
		lp: vanguard VRS 6016
		lp: chant du monde LDA 8111/LDX 8360
		lp: eurodisc XPK 88665/XAK 87695/ XDK 85645/XGK 86095
		lp: musical treasures MT 42
		cd: melodiya SUCD 10 00212/ CD10 00745/CD10 00741
		cd: rca/bmg 74321 341790/74321 407102
		cd: chant du monde LDC 278908
		cd: vanguard OCD 1024
		cd: dante LYS 354
		also issued by hispavox and opus
prague	prague radio	cd: praga PR 254 006/PR 256 007/PR 54006
22 may	orchestra	
1950	ancerl	

piano trio no 3

date	oborin, piano	lp: melodiya D 03560-03561/ D 028543-028544
uncertain	knushevitsky, cello	lp: westminster XWN 18176
		lp: monitor MC 2071
		cd: monitor MCD 27070
		cd: preiser 90593

piano trio no 4 "dumky"

date	oborin, piano	lp: melodiya D 03562-03563/ D 028561-028562
uncertain	knushevitsky, cello	lp: bruno 14009
		lp: colosseum CRLP 253
		lp: westminster XWN 18175
		lp: monitor MC 2070
		lp: eurodisc ZK 78419
		cd: monitor MCD 72070
		cd: preiser 90593

dvorak/**slavonic dance op 46 no 8**, arranged for violin and piano by press
warsaw	topilin, piano	lp: syrena 8601
1935		lp: masters of the bow MOB 1046
		this recording was not listed in world's encyclopedia of recorded music

MANUEL DE FALLA (1876-1946)
suite populaire espagnole, arranged by kochanski for violin and piano from the canciones populares espanoles
moscow	yampolsky, piano	lp: melodiya D 028807-028808/D 2163-2164
1953		cd: melodiya CD10 00745/CD10 00742
		cd: rca/bmg 74321 341802/74321 407102

jota/canciones populares espanoles, arranged for violin and piano
moscow	yampolsky, piano	lp: melodiya 18368-18369/00544-00545
31 august		lp: victor (japan) LS 2-25
1950		

london	yampolsky, piano	45: columbia SEL 1577/ESL 6252
28 february		45: columbia (italy) SEBQ 219/ESLQ 1007
1956		lp: columbia 33CX 1466/SAX 2253
		lp: columbia (france) SAXF 149
		lp: columbia (germany) WSX 604/SHZE 160
		lp: angel 35354/60259
		cd: testament SBT 1116
		cd: emi 562 9142
		also issued by melodiya, eterna, bruno and jvc

danza espanola/la vida breve, arranged for violin and piano by kreisler
moscow	yampolsky, piano	lp: melodiya 18368-18369
31 august		lp: bruno 14015
1950		lp: hall of fame HOF 519/HOFS 519
		lp: monitor MC 2003
		cd: monitor MCD 72003

GABRIEL FAURE (1845-1924)
piano quartet no 1
a recording of this work with gilels, oistrakh, terian and rostropovich was apparently listed in melodiya catalogues, but gilels discographies indicate that the participants were gilels, kogan, barshai and rostropovich

STEPHEN FOSTER (1826-1864)
old folks at home, arranged for violin and piano by kreisler
moscow	makarov, piano	78: melodiya 12458-12459
20 january		lp: colosseum CRLP 105
1945		*this recording was not listed in world's encyclopedia of recorded music*

CESAR FRANCK (1822-1890)
violin sonata in a

paris 1953	oborin, piano	lp: melodiya D 349-350/D 20574-20583 lp: colosseum CRLP 151 lp: vanguard VRS 6019 lp: chant du monde LDA 8112 cd: chant du monde LDC 278944 cd: vanguard OVC 4080-4082
stockholm june 1953	yampolsky, piano	lp: columbia 33CX 1201 lp: columbia (italy) QCX 10160 lp: columbia (france) FCX 355/FCX 30269/ FC 25042 lp: columbia (germany) WCX 1201/C 90389 lp: hmv (spain) LALP 497 lp: angel 35163
bucharest 1958	yampolsky, piano	vhs video: warner/nvc arts 8573 858013 dvd video: warner/nvc arts 8573 858012 *excerpt only*
paris 4 december 1968	richter, piano	cd: chant du monde LDC 278885

moscow
28 december
1968
	richter, piano	lp: melodiya D 025827-025828/
		   CM 02257-02258/C10 02257 005
		lp: emi ASD 2618/1C063 92240/
		   2C065 92240/3C065 92240
		lp: angel 40121
		lp: eurodisc KK 80080/300.609 420
		lp: chant du monde LDX 78444
		lp: eterna 826 214
		lp: musical heritage society MHS 3956
		lp: quintessence PMC 7133
		cd: vox CDX 5120
		cd: mobile fidelity MFCD 909
		cd: revelation RV 10048
		cd: rca/bmg 74321 341812/74321 407102
		cd: melodiya CD10 00745/CD10 00743
		revelation edition incorrectly dated 3 march 1966

ALEXANDER GLAZUNOV (1865-1936)
violin concerto

moscow	ussr state	78: ultraphon E 23871-23873
1948-1949	symphony	lp: melodiya D 012939-012940
	kondrashin	lp: supraphon LPM 7
		lp: colosseum CRLP 137
		lp: bruno 14013
		lp: period SHO 316/SPL 598
		lp: vanguard VRS 6005
		lp: monitor MC 2073
		lp: westminster WGM 8224
		lp: design DLP 134
		lp: chant du monde LDA 8041
		lp: classics club X 1037
		lp: gala GLP 372
		lp: eurodisc XGK 89511/XPK 88665
		cd: melodiya SUCD10 00239
		cd: dante LYS 331-334
		cd: monitor MCD 72073
		cd: vanguard OCD 1025

mazurka-oberek for violin and orchestra

date	moscow	lp: melodiya D 026211-026212/
uncertain	philharmonic	CM 02445-02446
	yudin	lp: colosseum CRLP 251
		lp: bruno 14012
		lp: westminster XWN 18177
		lp: monitor MC 2073
		cd: monitor MCD 72073
		cd: dante LYS 355
		this recording was not listed in world's encyclopedia of recorded music

méditation for violin and piano

date	yampolsky, piano	lp: melodiya D 1408-1409
uncertain		lp: colosseum CRLPX 011
		lp: vanguard VRS 6020
		cd: vanguard OVC 4080-4082

entr'acte from raymonda, arranged for violin and piano by rodionov

moscow	kollegorskaya,	lp: melodiya D 026333-026334
1951-1953	piano	cd: rca/bmg 74321 341802/74321 407102
		cd: melodiya CD10 00745/CD10 00742
		this recording was not listed in world's encyclopedia of recorded music

REINHOLD GLIERE (1875-1956)
romance in c, version for violin and orchestra

moscow	ussr state	lp: melodiya D 026211-026212
1947	symphony	lp: colosseum CRLP 149
	kondrashin	lp: vanguard VRS 6016
		cd: vanguard OCD 1025
		cd: melodiya SUCD10 00242
		cd: dante LYS 491-494

romance in c, version for violin and piano

moscow	kollegorskaya,	lp: melodiya D 026335-026336
1948		*this recording was not listed in world's encyclopedia of recorded music*

the bronze horseman, excerpts from the ballet

date	bolshoi theatre	78: melodiya 16342-16345
uncertain	orchestra	78: supraphon B 40116-40117
	gliere	lp: colosseum CRLP 179

MIKHAIL GLINKA (1803-1857)
persian song from russlan and lyudmila, arranged for violin and piano

date	topilin, piano	78: melodiya 10499-10500
uncertain		lp: colosseum CRLP 105

piano trio in d "trio pathétique"

date	oborin, piano	lp: melodiya
uncertain	knushevitsky,	lp: monitor MC 2068
	cello	lp: concert hall CHS 1306
		lp: colosseum CRLP 104

CHRISTOPH WILLIBALD GLUCK (1714-1787)
dance of the blessed spirits from orfeo ed euridice, arranged for violin and piano by kreisler

moscow	yampolsky, piano	cd: rca/bmg 74321 341802/74321 407102
1947		cd: melodiya CD10 00745/CD10 00742
		this recording was not listed in world's encyclopedia of recorded music

BENJAMIN GODARD (1849-1895)
canzonetta from violin concerto no 1
moscow	ussr state	lp: melodiya D 26211-26212
13 december	symphony	cd: melodiya SUCD10 00219
1948	kondrashin	cd: revelation RV 10015
		cd: dante LYS 492-494

this recording was not listed in world's encyclopedia of recorded music

canzonetta from violin concerto no 1, version for violin and piano
moscow	topilin, piano	78: melodiya 10497-10498
11 september		lp: colosseum CRLP 105
1949		

ENRIQUE GRANADOS (1867-1916)
andaluza from danzas espanolas, arranged for violin and piano by kreisler
moscow	makarov, piano	cd: rca/bmg 74321 407102/74321 341802
1947		cd: melodiya CD10 00745/CD10 00742

EDVARD GRIEG (1843-1907)
violin sonata no 1
moscow	oborin, piano	lp: melodiya D 012865-012866
5 january		lp: bruno 14038
1957		lp: mgm (usa) GC 30004
		cd: revelation RV 10016

violin sonata no 2
moscow	oborin, piano	lp: melodiya D 04880-04881
1958		lp: eurodisc ZK 78437

prague	bauer, piano	cd: praga PR 250 048/PR 256 007
2 may		
1972		

GEORGE FRIDERIC HANDEL (1685-1759)
sonata in g for two violins and keyboard

moscow 1950	beckman- scherbina, harpsichord i.oistrakh, second violin	lp: melodiya D 011075-011076 *this recording was not listed in world's encyclopedia of recorded music*
leipzig april 1957	yampolsky, piano i.oistrakh, second violin	45: dg EPL 30 287 lp: dg LP 16 136 lp: dg heliodor 89 561/478 132 lp: eterna 720 037/820 283 lp: decca (usa) DL 9962 lp: heliodor (usa) H 25009/HS 25009 cd: dg 463 6162
moscow 1959	ginsburg, piano i.oistrakh, second violin	lp: melodiya D 5670-5671/D 015349-015350 lp: hall of fame HOF 516/HOFS 516

water music suite

moscow 1959	moscow philharmonic *oistrakh conducts from the violin*	lp: melodiya SM 03343-03344 lp: chant du monde LDX 78564

FRANZ JOSEF HAYDN (1732-1809)
andante and presto from string quartet in b flat, arranged for violin and piano

paris march 1961	i.oistrakh, second violin	lp: melodiya D 14141-14142/S 0579-0580 lp: chant du monde LDXA 8280 lp: monitor MC 2058 lp: concert hall SMSC 201 cd: chant du monde LDC 278906 cd: notablu 93.5107

piano trio no 21

moscow 1950	oborin, piano knushevitsky, cello	lp: melodiya D 03822-03823 lp: colosseum CRLP 248 lp: monitor MC 2017 lp: westminster XWN 18176 *final movement only* 78: melodiya 18005-18006
prague 26 may 1961	oborin, piano knushevitsky, cello	cd: multisonic 31.0105

haydn/**piano trio no 28**
moscow	oborin, piano	lp: melodiya D 1311-1312/M10 48854 000
1951	knushevitsky, cello	lp: monitor MC 2059

PAUL HINDEMITH (1895-1963)
violin concerto

moscow	ussr state	lp: melodiya D 010977-010978/S 0661-0662
25 february	symphony	lp: chant du monde LDXA 48333
1962	rozhdestvensky	lp: mk records DO 10977
		lp: emi 1C063 63670
		lp: eurodisc XGK 89515/XPK 88665
		cd: melodiya SUCD10 00479
		cd: revelation RV 10075
		cd: chant du monde LDC 278941
		cd: forlane UCD 16589
		cd: urania (usa) US 5157
		recorded at the russian premiere of the concerto

london	london	lp: decca LXT 6035/SXL 6035/SDD 465
13-14	symphony	lp: london (usa) CM 9337/CS 6337
september	hindemith	cd: decca 414 4372/433 0812/470 2582
1962		

violin sonata in e flat
moscow	yampolsky, piano	lp: melodiya D 03822-03823
1956		lp: monitor MC 2009

ARTHUR HONEGGER (1892-1955)
sonatina for two violins
paris	i.oistrakh,	lp: melodiya D 14141-14142/S 0579-0580
24 march	second violin	lp: chant du monde LDXA 8280
1961		lp: monitor MC 2058
		lp: concert hall SMSC 201
		cd: chant du monde 278944

JENO HUBAY (1858-1937)
zephyr for violin and piano
moscow	topilin, piano	78: melodiya 10500-10501
11 september		lp: colosseum CRLP 105
1940		

LEOS JANACEK (1854-1928)
violin sonata
moscow	bauer, piano	lp: melodiya CM 01927-01928
1966		lp: chant du monde LDX 78489
		lp: eurodisc XPK 79289
		lp: westminster WGM 8292

DMITRY KABALEVSKY (1904-1987)
violin concerto

moscow	ussr state	78: melodiya 17231-17236
12 may	symphony	78: supraphon C 23041-23043
1949	kabalevsky	lp: melodiya D 489-490/D 3567-3568/ D 014029-014030
		lp: bruno 14001
		lp: colosseum CRLP 123
		lp: chant du monde LDXA 8082/LD 8003
		lp: monarch MWL 330
		lp: vanguard VRS 6002
		lp: monitor MC 2073
		lp: westminster XWN 18177
		cd: vanguard OCD 1025
		cd: monitor MCD 72073
		cd: chant du monde LDC 278883
		cd: dante LYS 356
		cd: revelation RV 10103

impromptu for violin and piano

date uncertain	yampolsky, piano	lp: melodiya D 022226-022227

ARAM KHACHATURIAN (1903-1978)
violin concerto

moscow	ussr state	78: melodiya 014151-014160
november	symphony	78: supraphon B 40058-40062
1942	gauk	78: ultraphon H 24098-24103
		78: decca K 1082-1086
		78: mercury DM 10
		lp: mercury MG 10000
		lp: period SPL 709
		cd: dante LYS 331-334
		cd: pearl GEMMCD 9295
		pearl edition is dated 1944

prague	prague radio	cd: multisonic 31.0038
15 may	orchestra	cd: praga PR 250 017/PR 256 007/PR 50017
1947	kubelik	

khachaturian/violin concerto/concluded

london	philharmonia	lp: columbia 33CX 1303
26-27	khachaturian	lp: columbia (italy) QCX 10188
november		lp: columbia (france) FCX 511/FCX 30291
1954		lp: columbia (germany) WCX 1303/C 90466
		lp: angel 35244
		cd: emi CDC 555 0352
moscow	ussr large radio	lp: melodiya D 016483-016488/
13 august	orchestra	S 01115-01116/SM 04375-04376
1965	khachaturian	lp: emi ASD 2472/3C065 93445
		lp: angel 40002
		lp: columbia (usa) Y-34068
		lp: eterna 826 163
		lp: eurodisc KK 74011/XGK 89511/ XPK 88665
		cd: mobile fidelity MFCD 899
		cd: chant du monde LDC 278883
		cd: russian disc RDCD 11012
		cd: vox CDX 5120
		cd: zyx melodiya 46123

an earlier version of the concerto conducted by the composer and listed in world's encyclopedia of recorded music is probably performed by leonid kogan

dance in b flat for violin and piano

moscow	yampolsky, piano	78: melodiya 14248-14249
1948		lp: colosseum CRLP 105/CRLP 249
		lp: vanguard VRS 6020
		lp: eurodisc CK 40444
		lp: chant du monde LDA 8075
		cd: chant du monde LDC 278945
		cd: vanguard OVC 4080-4082

some editions name the pianist as makarov or oborin

song poem in e for violin and piano

moscow	yampolsky, piano	78: melodiya 14246-14247
1948		78: supraphon B 40040
		lp: vanguard VRS 6020
		lp: chant du monde LDA 8075

KAREN KHACHATURIAN (born 1920)
violin sonata in g

brussels	yampolsky, piano	lp: columbia 33CX 1342
21 may		lp: columbia (italy) QCX 10202
1955		lp: columbia (france) FCX 514/FCX 30012
		lp: angel 35306
		lp: melodiya D 024427-024448
		lp: colosseum CRLP 252
		lp: bruno 14006
		cd: testament SBT 1113

ZOLTAN KODALY (1882-1967)
hungarian folk dances, arranged for violin and piano by feigin

moscow	yampolsky, piano	lp: melodiya D 029743-029744/D 5028-5029/
1953		lp: supraphon LPM 237/DM 5552/ SUEC 807/MKS 25007
		lp: colosseum CRLP 249
		lp: parliament PLP 118
		lp: eurodisc XA 85315
		lp: monitor MC 2003
		cd: monitor MCD 72003
berlin ddr	n.walter, piano	78: eterna 120 021
february		45: eterna 520 026
1954		lp: eterna LPM 1023/720 048
		lp: saga FID 1005
		cd: berlin classics BC 21322
london	yampolsky, piano	lp: columbia 33CX 1466/SAX 2253
18 february		lp: columbia (france) SAXF 149
1956		lp: columbia (germany) WSX 604/SHZE 160
		lp: angel 35354/60259
		cd: emi CDM 769 3672/562 9142

ZINOVI KOMPANEYETZ
ballade for violin and piano

moscow	topilin, piano	78: melodoya 7593-7594
31 october		*this recording was not listed in world's encyclopedia*
1938		*of recorded music*

FRITZ KREISLER (1875-1962)
variations on a theme of corelli in the style of tartini

moscow	makarov, piano	78: melodiya 044732-044733
1946		78: supraphon G 22207
		78: ultraphon G 14742
		45: mercury EP 15008
		lp: mercury MG 10035
		lp: colosseum CRLP 110

short filmed extract from this piece on warner/nvc arts vhs video 3984 230303 and dvd video 3984 230302

la gitana for violin and piano

moscow	yampolsky, piano	78: melodiya 17546-17547
10 december		lp: decca (usa) DL 9882
1949		lp: chant du monde LDA 8175/LDXSP 1801
		cd: chant du monde LDC 278945
		this recording was not listed in world's encyclopedia
		of recorded music

liebesleid for violin and piano

moscow	unnamed pianist	dvd video: emi classic archive DVB 599 6859
1937		*extract*
		vhs video: warner/nvc arts 3894 230303
		dvd video: warner/nvc arts 3894 230302

la précieuse in the style of couperin

moscow	yampolsky, piano	78: melodiya 17546-17547
10 december		*this recording was not listed in world's encyclopedia*
1949		*of recorded music*

rondino on a theme of beethoven

moscow	topilin, piano	78: melodiya 7591-7592
31 october		*this recording was not listed in world's encyclopedia*
1938		*of recorded music*

EDOUARD LALO (1823-1892)
symphonie espagnole pour violon et orchestre

moscow 23 january 1948	ussr state symphony kondrashin	78: melodiya 015565-015572 78: supraphon H 24094-24097/ 40138-40141 lp: colosseum CRLP 179 lp: bruno 14003 lp: design DLP 151 lp: hall of fame HOF 502/HOFS 502 lp: period SHO 312/SHOST 312 lp: eurodisc XAK 86039 lp: musidisc RC 818 lp: fidelio ATL 4020 lp: allegro ALL 708 lp: delta TQD 3002 cd: dante LYS 331-334 *fidelio edition named conductor as gauk*
moscow 1953	yampolsky, piano	vhs video: warner/nvc arts 3894 230303 dvd video: warner/nvc arts 3894 230302 dvd video: emi classic archive DVB 599 6859 *third movement only*
london 13-14 november 1954	philharmonia martinon	lp: columbia 33CX 1246 lp: columbia (italy) QCX 10151 lp: columbia (france) FCX 427 lp: columbia (germany) WCX 1246/C 90420 lp: angel 35205/60332 lp: emi XLP 30109 cd: testament SBT 1116

JEAN-MARIE LECLAIR (1697-1764)
violin sonata op 9 no 3

paris 19 june 1953	yampolsky, piano	lp: melodiya D 028113-028114/D 5604-5605 lp: colosseum CRLP 153 lp: vanguard VRS 6024 lp: chant du monde LDA 8075/LDXSP 1801 lp: eurodisc XA 85315/EK 70600 lp: musical appreciation society MAR 572 lp: concert hall M 2226 cd: vanguard OVC 4080-4082
berlin ddr february 1954	n.walter, piano	78: eterna 120 022-120 023 45: eterna 520 001 lp: eterna LPM 1023/720 048 cd: berlin classics BC 21322
tokyo 7-8 march 1955	yampolsky, piano	lp: victor LM 1787/VICS 1058/ALK1-4498 lp: victor (japan) LS 2026/RCX 1041 lp: victor (france) A630358R lp: hmv ALP 1411

ZARA LEVINA (born 1906)
violin sonata

moscow 1948	levina, piano	lp: melodiya M10 38010 000

YURI ABRAMOVICH LEVITIN (born 1912)
violin sonata

moscow 1959	levitin, piano	lp: melodiya D 05622-05623

PIETRO LOCATELLI (1695-1764)
violin sonata in f minor, arranged by ysaye

tokyo 7-8 march 1955 `	yampolsky, piano	lp: victor LM 1987/VICS 1058/ALK1-4498 lp: victor (japan) LS 2026/RCX 1017 lp: victor (france) A630358R lp: hmv ALP 1411 lp: colosseum CRLP 248

capriccio in d for solo violin

19 february 1972	lp: masters of the bow MOB 1046

capriccio in d, arranged for violin and orchestra by rozhdestvensky

moscow 27 september 1968	moscow philharmonic rozhdestvensky	dvd video: emi classic archive DVB 599 6859

NIKOLAI MEDTNER (1879-1951)
violin sonata no 3 "sonata epica"

moscow	goldenweiser,	lp: melodiya D 05596-05597
1959	piano	lp: eurodisc ZK 79839
		cd: dante HPC 149

nocturne for violin and piano

moscow	yampolsky, piano	lp: monitor MC 2003
14 august		cd: monitor MCD 72003
1947		

FELIX MENDELSSOHN-BARTHOLDY (1809-1847)
violin concerto

moscow	ussr state	78: melodiya 017327-017333
1949	symphony	lp: melodiya D 012939-012 940/D 1167-1168
	kondrashin	lp: colosseum CRLP 225
		lp: bruno 14011
		lp: hall of fame HOF 503/HOFS 503
		lp: period SHO 315/SHOST 315
		lp: musidisc RC 812
		lp: eurodisc XPK 88665/300.159 435
		lp: design DLP 134
		lp: vox PL 16160/GBY 10160
		lp: fidelio ATL 4007
		lp: delta TQD 3002
		lp: everest SDBR 3342
		lp: westminster WGM 8224
		cd: rca/bmg GD 69085
		cd: dante LYS 331-334
		cd: marble classics 91.0034

some lp editions incorrectly named conductor as gauk; also issued by hispavox, murray hill, arkadia and supermajestic

philadelphia	philadelphia	lp: columbia (usa) ML 5085/M 22219
24 december	orchestra	lp: philips ABL 3145/GBR 6507/A02149L/
1955	ormandy	G05602R
		lp: cbs 72306

opening section of the concerto with oistrakh and unnamed orchestra and conductor appears in a filmed extract in warner/nvc arts vhs video 8573 858013 and dvd video 8573 858012

mendelssohn/**piano trio no 1**
moscow	oborin, piano	lp: melodiya CM 02087-02088
1948	knushevitsky,	cd: chant du monde LDC 278943
	cello	cd: dante LYS 367
		first movement
		lp: melodiya D 18776-18777
		this recording was not listed in world's encyclopedia of recorded music

piano trio no 2
moscow	oborin, piano	lp: melodoya CM 02087-02088/
1948	knushevitsky,	D 01750-01751
	cello	lp: bruno 14053
		lp: eurodisc ZK 79841
		cd: chant du monde LDC 278943
		cd: dante LYS 371
		also issued by colosseum

auf flügeln des gesanges, arranged for violin and piano
moscow	yampolsky, piano	78: melodiya 017548-017549
10 december		lp: columbia (usa) ML 5096
1949		lp: monitor MC 2042
		cd: monitor MCD 72003
		this recording was not listed in world's encyclopedia of recorded music

canzonetta from string quartet op 12
moscow	bondarenko,	78: melodiya 018328-018329
7 august	second violin	
1950	terian, viola	
	knushevitsky,	
	cello	

ERNST HERMANN MEYER (born 1905)
violin concerto
berlin ddr	staatskapelle	lp: eterna 820 363
1964	suitner	lp: eterna nova 885 057

NIKOLAI MIASKOVSKY (1881-1950)
violin concerto

moscow	ussr state	78: melodiya 09660-09663 and 09676-09681
21-23	symphony	78: supraphon 40050-40054
september	gauk	78: ultraphon H 23885-23889
1939		78: decca X 272-276
		lp: colosseum CRLP 149
		lp: period SPL 539
		lp: musical heritage society 9014
		cd: dante LYS 331-334
		cd: pearl GEMMCD 9295

MORITZ MOSKOWSKI (1854-1925)
guitarre, arranged for violin and piano by sarasate

moscow	makarov, piano	78: melodiya 5519-5520
10 august		*this recording was not listed in world's encyclopedia*
1937		*of recorded music*

an undated extract from the work played by oistrakh is featured on warner/nvc arts vhs video 3984 230303 and dvd video 3984 230302

WOLFGANG AMADEUS MOZART (1756-1791)
violin concerto no 1 k207

moscow	moscow	cd: rca/bmg 74321 729142
2 february	philharmonic	
1963	kondrashin	
paris	orchestre	lp: philips AL 3455/SAL 3455/A02315L/
1963	lamoureux	835 190AY/6570 058
	haitink	lp: philips (usa) PHM 500 050/PHS 900 050
		lp: melodiya D 013725-013726/S 0865-0866
		lp: supraphon 11 1042 2125
		cd: philips 434 1672
berlin brd	berlin	lp: emi SLS 828/1C165 02323-02326
22-23	philharmonic	lp: angel 3789
march	*oistrakh conducts*	lp: melodiya SM 03883-03884
1971	*from the violin*	lp: eterna 826 478
		cd: emi CDM 769 1762/CDZ 479 5312/
		CZS 569 5422

mozart/**violin concerto no 2 k211**
berlin brd	berlin	lp: emi SLS 828/1C165 02323-02326
11-13	philharmonic	lp: angel 3789/32147
september	*oistrakh conducts*	lp: melodiya SM 03883-03884
1971	*from the violin*	lp: eterna 826 478
		cd: emi CDM 769 1762/CDZ 479 5312/ CZS 569 5422

violin concerto no 3 k216

prague	czech	lp: supraphon LPV 244/SUA 10127/ 010 2372/11 0582
27 april	philharmonic	
1954	ancerl	lp: eterna 820 565
		cd: supraphon SU 1936 2011/SU 3678 2001

london	philharmonia	lp: columbia 33CX 1660/SAX 2304
22 may	*oistrakh conducts*	lp: columbia (italy) QCX 10355/SAXQ 7315
1958	*from the violin*	lp: columbia (france) FC 25125
		lp: angel 35714/60233
		lp: emi XLP 30086/SXLP 30086/SHZE 152/ SMVP 802/SREG 1090/1C047 50510
		cd: emi CZS 569 3312
		oistrakh's first recorded assignment as a conductor due to sudden indisposition of alceo galliera

moscow	moscow chamber	lp: melodiya D 06129-06130/S 6655-6656
1959	orchestra	lp: artia ALP 156
	barshai	lp: bruno 14023
		lp: eurodisc XK 80569
		bruno edition names orchestra and conductor as moscow philharmonic and kondrashin

lugano	swiss-italian	cd: ermitage ERM 162
11 june	radio orchestra	
1961	nussio	

berlin brd	berlin	lp: emi SLS 828/1C165 02323-02326
22-23	philharmonic	lp: angel 3789/34709
march	*oistrakh conducts*	lp: melodiya SM 03885-03886
1971	*from the violin*	lp: eterna 826 479
		cd: emi CDM 769 1762/CDZ 479 5312/ CZS 569 5422

mozart/**violin concerto no 4 k218**

date uncertain	ussr state symphony kondrashin	lp: melodiya D 1562-1563 lp: colosseum CRLP 246 lp: bruno 14023 lp: classic editions (usa) CE 3002
philadelphia 14 december 1955	philadelphia orchestra ormandy	lp: columbia (usa) ML 5085/M 33328 lp: philips ABL 3145/GBR 6506/A01249L/ G05601R/S06633R lp: melodiya D 17385-17386/M10 46431 000 lp: cbs 72306
london 12 october 1965	moscow philharmonic kondrashin	cd: bbc legends BBCL 41272
berlin brd 23-24 november 1970	berlin philharmonic *oistrakh conducts from the violin*	lp: emi SLS 828/1C165 03423-02326 lp: angel 36894/3789/32104/34709 lp: melodiya SM 03885-03886 lp: eterna 826 479 cd: emi CDM 769 0642/CDM 764 8682 cd: laserlight 16220

filmed rehearsal extract of a performance with oistrakh in budapest in 1971 appears on warner/ nvc arts vhs video 3984 230303 and dvd video 3984 230302

mozart/**violin concerto no 5 k219**

moscow 1947	bolshoi theatre orchestra golovanov	lp: melodiya lp: colosseum CRLP 154 lp: period SHO 327/SPL 590 lp: musical heritage society 9013 lp: musidisc RC 822 cd: melodiya SUCD10 00230 cd: preludio PHC 2149 cd: tuxedo TUXCD 1052 cd: dante LYS 491-494 *some editions incorrectly dated and conductor named variously as gauk or kondrashin*
dresden 10-11 february 1954	staatskapelle dresden konwitschny	lp: dg LP 16 101/LPE 17 159/2700 111/ 2726 087 lp: dg heliodor 89 593/89 778/478 132 lp: eterna LPM 1016/720 030/820 004 lp: decca (usa) DL 9766/DX 141 lp: heliodor (usa) H 25017/HS 25017 cd: berlin classics BC 21312/BC 02172
berlin ddr 17 september 1955	staatskapelle konwitschy	cd: weitblick (japan) SSS 00192 *concert marking opening of the re-built deutsche staatsoper unter den linden*
new york 1 january 1956	new york philharmonic mitropoulos	cd: arkadia CDMP 418/CDLSMH 34018 cd: as-disc AS 502 cd: one eleven URS 50140 cd: disc (greece) 189 6172
vienna 21 june 1956	leningrad philharmonic mravinsky	cd: cetra CDAR 2034/CDE 1025 cd: stradivarius STR 10005 cd: notablu 93.5107 *stradivarius and notablu editions incorrectly dated*
berlin brd 23-24 november 1970	berlin philharmonic *oistrakh conducts from the violin*	lp: emi SLS 828/1C165 02323-02326 lp: angel 36894/3789/32104/34709 lp: melodiya SM 03887-03888 lp: eterna 826 480 cd: emi CMS 763 6012/CDM 764 0642/ CDM 764 8682 cd: laserlight 16220
berlin brd september 1972	european youth orchestra karajan	lp: melodiya C10 17501-17504

mozart/**violin concerto no 7 k271a**

date	ussr state	lp: melodiya D 1562-1563
uncertain	symphony	lp: colosseum CRLP 154
	kondrashin	lp: classic editions (usa) CE 3002
		cd: melodiya SUCD10 00230

sinfonia concertante for violin and viola k364

moscow	moscow chamber	lp: melodiya D 05236-053237
1960	orchestra	lp: artia ALP 165
	oistrakh, violin	lp: musidisc RC 859
	barshai, viola	lp: period SHO 343/SHOST 343
	barshai conducts	lp: vedette VSC 4020
	from the viola	lp: eurodisc ZK 77293
		lp: recital hall RH 301
		lp: musical masterpoece society MMS 2272
		lp: chant du monde LDP 8248/LDX 78698
		cd: chant du monde LDC 278906
london	moscow	cd: bbc legends BBCL 40192
28 september	philharmonic	*excerpt*
1963	menuhin	vhs video: warner/nvc arts 3984 230303
	i.oistrakh, violin	dvd video: warner/nvc arts 3984 230302
	oistrakh, viola	dvd video: emi classic archive DVA 490 4499
london	moscow	lp: decca LXT 6088/SXL 6088/SDD 445
september	philharmonic	lp: london (usa) CM 9377/CS 6377/STS 15482
1963	kondrashin	cd: decca 417 7592
	i.oistrakh, violin	
	oistrakh, viola	
berlin brd	berlin	lp: emi SLS 828/1C165 02323-02326
8-10	philharmonic	lp: angel 3789/32147
march	i.oistrakh, violin	lp: melodiya SM 03887-03888
1972	oistrakh, viola	lp: eterna 826 481
	oistrakh conducts	cd: emi CDM 764 6322/CDM 769 6532
	from the viola	
vienna	vienna	lp: melodiya C10 25415-25416
28 may	philharmonic	
1972	i.oistrakh, violin	
	oistrakh, viola	
	oistrakh conducts	
	from the viola	

mozart/**concertone for two violins k190**
berlin brd	berlin	lp: emi SLS 828/1C165 02323-02326
8-10	philharmonic	lp: angel 3789
march	i.oistrakh,	lp: melodiya SM 03889-03890
1972	second violin	lp: eterna 826 481
	oistrakh conducts	cd: emi CDM 769 6532
	from the violin	

adagio for violin and orchestra k261
berlin brd	berlin	lp: emi SLS 828/1C165 02323-02326
11-13	philharmonic	lp: angel 3789
september	*oistrakh conducts*	lp: melodiya SM 03887-03888
1971	*from the violin*	lp: eterna 826 480
		cd: emi CDM 769 6532/CDM 764 8682

rondo for violin and orchestra k269
berlin brd	berlin	lp: emi SLS 828/1C165 02323-02326
11-13	philharmonic	lp: angel 3789
september	*oistrakh conducts*	lp: melodiya SM 03887-03888
1971	*from the violin*	lp: eterna 826 480
		cd: emi CDM 769 6532/CDM 764 8682

rondo for violin and orchestra k373
berlin brd	berlin	lp: emi SLS 828/1C165 02323-02326
11-13	philharmonic	lp: angel 3789
september	*oistrakh conducts*	lp: melodiya SM 03887-03888
1971	*from the violin*	lp: eterna 826 480
		cd: emi CDM 769 6532/CDM 764 8682/
		CZS 569 5422

violin sonata no 23 k306
vienna	badura-skoda,	lp: victor SER 5681-5682
june-	piano	lp: eurodisc XRK 27315/300.613 435
september		lp: melodiya SM 03961-03962
1972		lp: chant du monde LDX 7855-7856
		cd: chant du monde LDC 2780909

violin sonata no 25 k377
vienna	badura-skoda,	lp: eurodisc 300.613 435
june-	piano	lp: melodiya SM 03963-03964/S10 25415-25416
september		lp: chant du monde LDX 7855-7856
1972		

mozart/**violin sonata no 27 k379**
date uncertain	oborin, piano	lp: melodiya D 012849-012850
		lp: colosseum CRLP 194
		lp: monarch MWL 334
		lp: concertone/halo 20222/50222
vienna june-september 1972	badura-skoda, piano	lp: eurodisc 300.613 435
		lp: melodiya SM 03961-03962/S10 25415-25416

violin sonata no 32 k454
moscow 1950	yampolsky, piano	lp: melodiya D 06335-06336
		lp: colosseum CRLP 194
		lp: monarch MWL 334
		lp: monitor MC 2005
london 16 february 1956	yampolsky, piano	lp: columbia 33CX 1415
		lp: columbia (italy) QCX 10306
		lp: columbia (france) FCX 654
		lp: columbia (germany) WCX 1415/C 90529
		lp: hmv (spain) LALP 475
		lp: angel 35356
		lp: melodiya D 012865-012866
		lp: emi 1C147 52238-52239
		cd: testament SBT 1115
vienna june-september 1972	badura-skoda, piano	lp: victor SER 5681-5682
		lp: eurodisc 300.613 435
		lp: melodiya SM 03963-03964/S10 25415-25416
		lp: chant du monde LDX 7855-7856
		cd: chant du monde LDC 278909

violin sonata no 33 k481
vienna june-september 1972	badura-skoda, piano	lp: victor SER 5681-5682
		lp: eurodisc 300.613 435
		lp: melodiya SM 03963-03964/S10 25415-25416
		lp: chant du monde LDX 7855-7856
		cd: chant du monde LDC 278909

mozart/**duo for violin and viola k423**
london	i.oistrakh, viola	lp: decca LXT 6088/SXL 6088
september		lp: london (usa) CM 9377/CS 6377/STS 15482
1963		cd: decca 430 1222

duo for violin and viola k424
date	i.oistrakh, violin	lp: melodiya D 32256-3227
uncertain		

variations on la bergere celimene
prague	bauer, piano	cd: praga PR 254 019/PR 256 007
17 july		
1972		

vienna	badura-skoda,	lp: eurodisc 300.615 435
june-	piano	
september		
1972		

variations on j'ai perdu mon amant
vienna	badura-skoda,	lp: eurodisc 300.615 435
june-	piano	
september		
1972		

clarinet quintet k581
date	sorokin, clarinet	lp: melodiya D 9135-9136
uncertain	bondarenko,	cd: doremi DHR 7702
	second violin	
	terian, viola	
	knushevitsky,	
	cello	

flute quartet k171
date	madatov, flute	lp: melodiya D 012849-012850
uncertain	terian, viola	
	knushevitsky,	
	cello	

NICCOLO PAGANINI (1782-1840)
caprice no 13 "le rire du diable", arranged for violin and piano by kreisler
moscow yampolsky, piano 78: melodiya 16285-16286
6 october   lp: colosseum CRLP 179
1948   lp: period SPL 710

caprice no 17 "andantino capriccioso"
moscow   78: melodiya 16339-16340
6 october   lp: colosseum CRLP 179
1948   lp: period SPL 710
filmed extract from this caprice appears on warner/nvc arts vhs video 3984 230303 and dvd video 3984 230302

variations on a theme from rossini's mosé for violin and piano
moscow yampolsky, piano lp: melodiya D 04044-04045
1951   lp: decca (usa) DL 9982
       lp: chant du monde LDA 8175/LDX 1801
       lp: classics club SMP 101
       lp: musidisc RC 858
       lp: concert hall MMS 2226
       lp: grandi musici GM 15
       cd: chant du monde LDC 278945
       cd: planeta (italy) GEP 14-2

berlin ddr yampolsky, piano lp: melodiya M10 46361 000
7 april
1952

SERGE PROKOFIEV (1891-1953)
violin concerto no 1

prague 15 may 1947	czech philharmonic kubelik	cd: multisonic 31.0038

moscow   ussr state   78: melodiya 015181-015186/
1947-1949   symphony   D 025326-026331
                  kondrashin   78: supraphon B 40015-40017
                                   78: ultraphon H 23947-23949
                                   lp: melodiya D 03040-03041
                                   lp: bruno 14002
                                   lp: colosseum CRLP 123
                                   lp: period SHO 338/SPL 739
                                   lp: monitor MC 2073
                                   lp: eurodisc ZK 78439
                                   lp: classics club X 1027
                                   lp: everest SDBR 3367
                                   lp: westminster XWN 18178
                                   lp: saga XID 5160
                                   cd: dante LYS 278/LYS 356
                                   cd: monitor MCD 62014
                                   cd: revelation RV 10074
                                   cd: melodiya SUCD 10 00242
                                   cd: yedang classics (japan)
                                   some editions contained incorrect attributions

london   london   lp: columbia 33CX 1268
18-20   symphony   lp: columbia (italy) QCX 10240
november   matacic   lp: columbia (france) FCX 419/FCX 30245
1954   lp: columbia (germany) WS 531/C 70430/
                                   C 91395
                                   lp: hmv (spain) LALP 255
                                   lp: angel 35243
                                   cd: testament SBT 1116
                                   cd: emi 562 8882

strassburg   strassburg   lp: grandi concerti GC 32
13 june   orchestra
1959   bour

prokofiev/violin concerto no 1/concluded

berlin ddr 8 march 1965	rundfunk- sinfonie-orchester sanderling	lp: melodiya M10 46419 000 cd: dante LYS 491-494
prague 1966	moscow philharmonic temirkanov	cd: praga PR 250 041/PR 256 007
amsterdam 8 october 1972	concertgebouw orchestra haitink	cd: q-disc (netherlands) 97014

violin concerto no 2

london 14-19 may 1958	philharmonia galliera	lp: columbia 33CX 1660/SAX 2304 lp: columbia (italy) QCX 10355/SAXQ 7315 lp: columbia (france) FCX 30249 lp: angel 35714/60223 lp: emi SLS 5004/SXLP 30155 cd: emi CZS 569 3312/562 8882

a version of the concerto issued by melodiya and bruno and conducted by kondrashin is thought to be performed by leonid kogan

prokofiev/**violin sonata no 1**

moscow 1947	oborin, piano	78: melodiya 014963-014970 lp: melodiya D 5552-5553 lp: colosseum CRLP 152 lp: chant du monde LDA 8078 lp: vanguard VRS 6019 cd: vanguard OVC 4080-4082 *vanguard editions are described as from paris 1953;* *world's encyclopedia of recorded music incorrectly* *attributed catalogue numbers 014963-014970 to* *a recording of violin sonata no 2 (error corrected in* *third supplement of werm)*
tokyo 7-8 march 1955	yampolsky, piano	lp: victor LM 1987/RB 16166/GM 43367 lp: victor (france) A 630358R lp: hmv ALP 1411 lp: melodiya D 024427-024428 lp: bruno 14006
prague 19 may 1966	bauer, piano	cd: praga PR 250 041/PR 256 007
moscow 1969	bauer, piano	lp: melodiya SM 01927-01928 lp: chant du monde LDX 78489 lp: eurodisc PK 79289 lp: westminster WGM 8292
moscow 19 march 1972	richter, piano	lp: melodiya S10 05003 007 lp: emi ASD 3105/3C065 97791 lp: angel 40268 lp: eurodisc MK 87954/XRK 27315 lp: supraphon 111 2175 lp: chant du monde C 5003 lp: musical heritage society MHS 4577 cd: zyx melodiya 46063
salzburg 20 august 1972	richter, piano	cd: deagostini FS96 CD29 cd: orfeo C489 981B

prokofiev/**violin sonata no 2**
brussels	yampolsky, piano	lp: columbia 33CX 1342
22 may		lp: columbia (italy) QCX 10202
1955		lp: columbia (france) FCX 514/FCX 30012
		lp: angel 35306
		lp: melodoya D 024427-024428
		lp: colosseum CRLP 252
		lp: bruno 14006
		cd: testament SBT 1113
		cd: emi 562 8882

sonata for two violins
moscow	i.oistrakh,	lp: melodiya 5670-5671/D 015349-015350
1959-1961	second violin	cd: revelation RV 10039
		cd: yedang classics (japan) CT 10031

moscow	i.oistrakh,	lp: melodiya D 14141-14142/S 0579-0580
march	second violin	lp: monitor MC 2058
1961		lp: chant du monde LDXA 8280
		lp: concert hall SMSC 201
		cd: chant du monde LDC 278910
		cd: art and electronics AED 68022

paris	i.oistrakh,	dvd video: emi classic archive DVA 492 6389
1962	second violin	*allegro movement only*

scherzo and march from the love of 3 oranges, arranged for violin and piano
berlin ddr	yampolsky, piano	lp: melodiya M10 46361-46362
7 april		lp: supraphon LPM 237/SUEC 807/
1952		MKS 25007
		lp: parliament PLP 118
		lp: monitor MC 2003
		cd: monitor MCD 72003

prokofiev/5 pieces from cinderella, arranged for violin and piano by fichtenholz

berlin ddr february 1954	n.walter, piano	lp: melodiya D 02794-02795 lp: eterna 120 025 lp: colosseum CRLP 110 lp: eurodisc CK 40442 lp: monarch MWL 707 lp: vanguard VRS 6020 lp: saga FID 1003/XID 5160 cd: vanguard OVC 4080-4082 *mazurka and winter fairy only* 78: ultraphon G 23287 *some editions incorrectly named pianist as yampolsky*

5 melodies for violin and piano

moscow 16 september 1947	yampolsky, piano	cd: revelation RV 10074
paris 29 march 1962	bauer, piano	dvd video: emi classic archive DVA 492 6389
paris 2 february 1966	bauer, piano	lp: philips SAL 3589/802 727AY/6570 206 lp: philips (usa) PHM 500 112/PHS 900 112 lp: melodiya D 020403-020404/ S 01527-01528 lp: chant du monde LDXS 78352 cd: chant du monde LDC 278910 cd: philips 420 7772
prague 18 may 1966	bauer, piano	cd: multisonic 31.0109 cd: praga PR 250 041/PR 256 007
moscow 18 september 1967	bauer, piano	lp: melodiya M10 46361-46362

5 melodies for violin and piano, nos 2 and 3 only

moscow 1947	makarov, piano	78: melodiya D 14633-14634 78: ultraphon G 14171 78: telefunken E 22206 78: mercury DM 27 78: chant du monde GA 5002 45: mercury EP 15008 lp: mercury MG 10035 lp: supraphon 11 051 lp: colosseum CRLP 110 *colosseum edition named pianist as yampolsky*

SERGEI RACHMANINOV (1873-1943)
piano trio no 2 "élégique"
moscow   oborin, piano   78: melodiya 019794-019805
1948   knushevitsky,   lp: melodiya D 04436-04437
                cello   lp: bruno 14077
                                   cd: mk MK 417111
                                   cd: preiser 90596
preiser edition suggests a recording date of 1958

romance for violin and piano op 6 no 1
moscow   yampolsky, piano   78: melodiya 1408-1409/17367-17368
27 october
1949

daisies, arranged for violin and piano by kreisler
moscow   yampolsky, piano   78: melodiya 1408-1409/17371-17372
27 october   cd: rca/bmg 74321 407102/74321 341802
1949   cd: melodiya CD10 00745/CD10 00742

vocalise, arranged for violin and piano
moscow   kollegorskaya,   45: mercury EP 15008
1947   piano   lp: colosseum CRLPX 011
                                   lp: vanguard VRS 6020
                                   cd: vanguard OVC 4080-4082
                                   cd: rca/bmg 74321 407102/74321 341802
                                   cd: melodiya CD10 00745/CD10 00742
this recording was not listed in world's encyclopedia of recorded music

NIKOLAI RAKOV (1908-1990)
violin concerto no 1

leningrad 1947	leningrad radio orchestra eliasberg	cd: revelation RV 10104 cd: dante LYS 491-494
moscow 1948	ussr state symphony kondrashin	78: melodiya 015368-015374 lp: melodiya D 2685-2686 lp: ultraphon 1667 lp: colosseum CRLP 002 lp: period SPL 709 lp: gallery (usa) LP 12001 lp: griffon 1004 *some editions incorrectly name conductor as gauk or rakov*

violin sonata

moscow 1953	rakov, piano	lp: melodiya D 02794-02795 *this recording was not listed in world's encyclopedia of recorded music*

poem for violin and piano

moscow 1948	rakov, piano	lp: melodiya D 05622-05623/ D 16477-16478

5 pieces for two violins and piano

date uncertain	rakov, piano pikaizen, second violin	lp: melodiya D 11055-11056 *this recording was not listed in world's encyclopedia of recorded music*

MAURICE RAVEL (1875-1937)
tzigane pour violon et orchestre

moscow 15 march 1948	ussr state symphony kondrashin	lp: melodiya D 03040-03041 lp: monitor MC 2073 lp: bruno 14009 lp: chant du monde LDM 8173/LDX 8359 lp: eurodisc XK 80569 lp: westminster WGM 8251/XWN 18177 cd: melodiya SUCD 10 00219 cd: chant du monde LDC 278908 cd: monitor MCD 72073 cd: dante LYS 356
date uncertain	ussr large radio orchestra rozhdestvensky	lp: melodiya D 021415-021416/ S 01617-01618

ravel/**tzigane, version for violin and piano**
prague 31 may 1957	yampolsky, piano	lp: chant du monde LDX 8359 cd: praga PR 254 016/PR 256 007

violin sonata in g
paris 4 april 1966	bauer, piano	lp: philips SAL 3589/802 727AY/6570 206 lp: philips (usa) PHM 500 112/PHS 900 112 lp: melodiya D 020403-020404/ S 01527-01528 lp: chant du monde LDX 78712/LDX 78362 cd: chant du monde LDC 278944 cd: philips 420 7772
prague 18 may 1966	bauer, piano	cd: multisonic 31.0109 cd: praga PR 254 016/PR 256 007/PR 54016
moscow 18 september 1967	bauer, piano	lp: melodiya M10 46361-46362

undated filmed extract from the sonata played by oistrakh on warner/ nvc arts vhs video 3984 230303 and dvd video 3984 230302

piano trio in a
moscow 1952	oborin, piano knushevitsky, cello	lp: melodiya D 2165-2166 lp: colosseum CRLP 252 lp: monitor MC 2069 lp: monarch MWL 367 lp: chant du monde LDM 8146 lp: eurodisc XK 79835 lp: westminster XWN 18174 cd: monitor MCD 72069 cd: chant du monde LDC 278907 cd: preiser 90596

NIKOLAI RIMSKY-KORSAKOV (1844-1908)
scheherazade, symphonic suite with violin solo

moscow	bolshoi theatre	78: melodiya 014691-014702
april	orchestra	78: supraphon B 40099-40104
1947	golovanov	78: ultraphon H 23935-23940
		lp: colosseum CRLP 135
		cd: arlecchino ARL 25/ARL 34
		cd: multisonic 31.0186
		cd: dante LYS 331-334
		cd: istituto discografico IDIS 6396
		some cd editions name conductor as anosov

piano trio in c

moscow	oborin, piano	lp: melodiya D 04524-04525/D 05542-05543
1952	knushevitsky,	lp: monarch MWL 317
	cello	lp: concert hall CHS 1306
		lp: westminster WGM 8321
		cd: chant du monde LDC 278907
		cd: preiser 90595

CAMILLE SAINT-SAENS (1835-1921)
introduction and rondo capriccioso for violin and orchestra

moscow	ussr state	78: melodiya 016274-016275
1947	symphony	78: ultraphon H 24271
	kondrashin	lp: colosseum CRLP 249
		lp: bruno 14018
		cd: melodiya SUCD10 00219
		cd: dante LYS 356

boston	boston	lp: victor LM 1988/RB 16166/VIC 1058/
14 december	symphony	VICS 1058/GM 43367
1955	munch	lp: victor (france) A630356R
		lp: hmv ALP 1460
		lp: melodiya D 021421-021422
		cd: rca/bmg GD 60683/09026 606832

étude en forme de valse, arranged for violin and piano by ysaye

date	yampolsky, piano	78: melodiya 021961-021962
uncertain		lp: melodiya D 04044-04045/D 1201-1202
		lp: colosseum CRLP 249
		lp: bruno 14018
		lp: hall of fame HOF 519/HOFS 519
		lp: fondation ysaye FEY 3001
		lp: monitor MC 2003
		cd: monitor MCD 72003

PABLO DE SARASATE (1844-1908)
navarra, spanish dance for two violins and orchestra

leipzig	gewandhaus-	45: dg EPL 30 286
17 april	orchester	45: eterna 520 119
1957	konwitschny	lp: dg heliodor 89 688/478 437
	i.oistrakh,	lp: eterna 720 048
	second violin	lp: decca (usa) DL 9962
		lp: melodiya D 026593-026594/ S10 17504 000
		cd: dg 459 0162/459 0672/463 6162

navarra, version for two violins and piano

moscow	yampolsky, piano	78: melodiya 6369-6370
1950	i.oistrakh,	lp: melodiya D 1201-1202/D 17637-17638/ D 029743-029744
	second violin	lp: monitor MC 2009
		lp: hall of fame HOF 516/HOFS 516

moscow	yampolsky, piano	cd: revelation RV 10039
21 may	i.oistrakh,	cd: yedang classics CT 10031
1954	second violin	

carmen fantasy for violin and piano

moscow	makarov, piano	78: melodiya 11659-11660
september		lp: colosseum CRLP 105
1943		lp: compass (usa) C 204

adios montanas mias, for violin and piano

moscow	yampolsky, piano	78: melodiya 19538-19539
1951		lp: melodiya D 1201-1202/D 028807-028808
		lp: colosseum CRLP 249
		lp: decca (usa) DL 9882
		lp: hall of fame HOF 519/HOFS 519
		lp: chant du monde LDM 8175
		cd: chant du monde LDC 278945

sarasate/**habanera and malaguena from danzas espanolas**
date yampolsky, piano lp: melodiya D 1188-1189/D 021758-021759
uncertain

zapateado from danzas espanolas
moscow makarov, piano 78: melodiya 12457-12458
20 january lp: colosseum CRLP 105
1945

FRANZ SCHUBERT (1797-1828)
duo in a for violin and piano d574
moscow oborin, piano lp: melodiya 04480-04481
1951 lp: colosseum CRLP 151
  lp: period SPL 573
  lp: monarch MWL 311
  lp: hall of fame HOF 503/HOFS 503
  lp: saga XID 5253
  lp: eurodisc XB 25428
  lp: chant du monde LDA 8108
  cd: new line OM 03109
  also published by dover and concertone/halo

paris oborin, piano dvd video: emi classic archive DVA 492 6389
27 june *andantino only*
1962

prague bauer, piano cd: multisonic 31.0109
18 may cd: praga PR 254 019/PR 256 007
1966

tours richter, piano lp: rococo 2097
2 july
1967

paris richter, piano cd: chant du monde LDC 278885
4 december
1968

moscow bauer, piano lp: melodiya SM 01925-01926
1969 lp: angel 40194
  lp: chant du monde LDX 78429
  lp: eurodisc XRK 27315

schubert/**fantasy in c for violin and piano d934**

moscow	bauer, piano	lp: melodiya SM 01925-01926
1969		lp: angel 40194
		lp: chant du monde LDX 78479
		lp: eurodisc XBK 25428

octet d803

london	bondarenko	lp: columbia 33CX 1423
27 october	terian	lp: columbia (france) FCX 30246
1955	knushevitsky	lp: hmv (spain) LALP 349
	sorokin	lp: angel 35362
	gertovich	lp: melodiya D 04926-04927/D 18661-18662
	stidel	cd: testament SBT 1113
	shapiro	

piano trio no 1 d898

moscow	oborin, piano	lp: melodiya M10 48853-48862
1947	knushevitsky,	cd: doremi DHR 7710
	cello	cd: dante LYS 367
		also issued by colosseum; this recording was not listed in world's encyclopedia of recorded music

london	oborin, piano	lp: columbia 33CX 1627/SAX 2281
13-16	knushevitsky,	lp: columbia (france) FCX 889/SAXF 161
may	cello	lp: columbia (germany) WSX 553/C 80543/
1958		SCXW 7519/STC 80543
		lp: angel 35713
		lp: world records CM 88
		lp: emi CFP 40037/1C047 01490
		cd: emi CZS 569 3672

prague	oborin, piano	cd: multisonic 31.0105
26 may	knushevitsky,	cd: praga PR 254 019/PR 256 007
1961	cello	

schubert/**piano trio no 2 d929**

moscow	oborin, piano	lp: melodiya D 05018-05019
1947	knushevitsky,	lp: eurodisc ZK 78423/XBK 25428
	cello	cd: doremi DHR 7710
		cd: preiser 90597
		cd: dante LYS 371
		this recording was not listed in world's encyclopedia of recorded music

piano quintet d667 "the trout"

moscow	oborin, piano	cd: new line OM 03109
1947	kaplun, viola	
	knushevitsky, cello	
	gertovich, double-bass	

andante from string quartet no 14 d810

date	bondarenko,	78: melodiya 00205-00208/018326-018329
uncertain	second violin	lp: classic editions (usa) CE 2
	terian, viola	cd: doremi DHR 7701
	knushevitsky, cello	

ROBERT SCHUMANN (1810-1856)
piano quartet in e flat

moscow	goldenweiser,	lp: chant du monde LDX 8142
1952	piano	
	terian, viola	
	knushevitsky, cello	

piano trio no 1

moscow	oborin, poano	cd: trition DMCC 24038
1948	knushevitsky, cello	

moscow	goldenweiser,	lp: chant du monde LDX 8142
1952	piano	
	knushevitsky, cello	

romanze in a, arranged for violin and piano by kreisler

moscow	makarov, piano	cd: rca.bmg 74321 407102/74321 341802
1947		cd: melodiya CD10 00745/CD10 00742

schumann/**widmung**, arranged for violin and piano by auer
warsaw	unnamed	78: syrena 8600
1935	pianist	

moscow	kollegorskaya,	cd: rca.bmg 74321 407102/74321 341802
1947	piano	cd: melodiya CD10 00745/CD10 00742
		this recording was not listed in world's encyclopedia of recorded music

filmed extract of a 1935 warsaw performance is on warner/nvc arts vhs video 3984 230303 and dvd video 38984 230302

ALEXANDER SCRIABIN (1872-1915)
étude in d flat, arranged for violin and piano by szigeti
moscow	grakov, piano	78: melodiya 5525-5526
13 august		78: decca M 545
1937		78: disc (usa) 4008

nocturne in f sharp minor, arranged for violin and piano by mogilevsky
moscow	grakov, piano	78: melodiya 5525-5526
13 august		78: decca M 545
1937		78: disc (usa) 4008
		cd: pearl GEMMCD 9440

moscow	makarov, piano	78: ultraphon G 14741
1947		78: supraphon G 22206
		78: telefunken E 22206
		78: mercury DM 27
		45: mercury EP 15008
		lp: mercury MG 10035
		lp: colosseum CRLP 110

moscow	yampolsky, piano	lp: melodiya D 5028-5029/D 028807-028808
1952		lp: monitor MC 2003
		cd: monitor MCD 72003

DIMITRI SHOSTAKOVICH (1906-1975)
violin concerto no 1
the concerto was given its first performance by david oistrakh and evgeny mravinsky in october 1955

new york 1 january 1956	new york philharmonic mitropoulos	lp: cetra DOC 6 cd: new york philharmonic NYOP 9701 *this was the new york premiere performance*
new york 2 january 1956	new york philharmonic mitropoulos	lp: columbia (usa) ML 5077/MG 33328 lp: philips ABL 3101/A01238L lp: cbs 77394 cd: sony MHK 63327/39771/SM2K 89317/ 517 1982
leningrad 30 november 1956	leningrad philharmonic mravinsky	lp: melodiya D 5540-5541/D 03658-03659/ D 033449-033552 lp: bruno 14017 lp: monitor MC 2014 lp: parlophone PMB 1014 lp: acropole APCC 60028 lp: period SHO 342/SHOST 2342 lp: telefunken TW 30213 lp: eurodisc ZK 79829/XPK 88665/ XGK 89511 lp: chant du monde LD 8186/LDX 8342 lp: emi SLS 5058 cd: monitor MCD 62014 cd: urania (usa) US 5171 cd: chant du monde LDC 278882 cd: rca/bmg GD 69084/74321 729142
prague may 1957	czech philharmonic mravinsky	cd: praga PR 250 052/PR 256 007
edinburgh 7 september 1962	philharmonia rozhdestvensky	cd: bbc radio classics 15656 91702 cd: bbc legends BBCL 40602 *second movement* cd: bbc worldwide TN 001
tokyo 18 april 1967	moscow philharmonic kondrashin	cd: altus (japan)
london 20 november 1972	new philharmonia m.shostakovich	cd: intaglio INCD 7241
london 25 november 1972	new philharmonia m.shostakovich	lp: emi ASD 2936/ASD 4040/1C069 02400/ 2C069 02400/3C065 02400 lp: angel 36964 lp: melodiya SM 04291-04292

filmed rehearsal extract for a 1960s performance of the concerto with oistrakh in berlin appears on warner/nvc arts vhs video 8573 858013 and 3984 230303 and dvd video 8573 858012 and 3984 230302

shostakovich/**violin concerto no 2**

moscow 13 september 1967	moscow philharmonic kondrashin	lp: melodiya D 021405-021406/S 01627-01628/ S10 06907-06908 lp: emi ASD 2447/2C069 94559/3C065 94559 lp: angel 40064 lp: eurodisc XPK 88665 lp: chant du monde LDX 78415 cd: chant du monde LDC 278882 cd: melodiya SUCD10 00242 cd: russian disc RDCD 11025 cd: rca/bmg GD 72914/74321 729142 *this was the world premiere performance of the concerto*
london august 1968	ussr state symphony svetlanov	cd: intaglio INCD 7241 cd: bbc legends BBCL 40602
moscow 27 september 1968	moscow philharmonic rozhdestvensky	lp: melodiya S10 17502-17503

filmed extract from one of the above performances appears on warner/nvc arts vhs video 3984 230303 and dvd video 3984 230302

shostakovich/**violin sonata**
moscow 1968	shostakovich, piano	lp: melodiya M10 42045-42046 cd: revelation RV 10008

moscow
3 may
1969
	richter, piano	lp: melodiya D 027313-027314/
		    SM 02355-02356/S10 02355 006
		lp: eterna 826 599
		lp: emi ASD 2718/HQS 1369/2C069 99149/
		    3C065 99149
		lp: angel 40189
		lp: eurodisc XMK 80531
		cd: chant du monde LDC 278 1018-1019
		cd: mobile fidelity MFCD 909
		cd: vox CDX 5120
		cd: rca/bmg 74321 341822/74321 407102
		cd: melodiya CD10 00745/CD10 00744

piano trio no 2
prague may 1946	shostakovich, piano sadlo, cello	78: supraphon G 22667-22669 78: ultraphon G 14927-14929 78: eurochord TAI 721-723 78: mercury DM 21 lp: colosseum CRLPX 011 lp: mercury MG 10045 lp: eurodisc 300.267 420 cd: doremi DHR 7701
moscow 1960	oborin, piano knushevitsky, cello	cd: trition DMCC 26018
prague 1961	oborin, piano knushevitsky, cello	cd: multisonic 31.0105 cd: praga PR 254 054/PR 256 007

seven romances on verses by alexander blok, for soprano and piano trio
moscow 23 october 1967	vishnevskaya vainberg, piano rostropovich, cello	cd: revelation RV 10101 cd: rca/bmg 74321 523372 *this was the world premiere performance*

JEAN SIBELIUS (1865-1957)
violin concerto

moscow 1946-1947	ussr state symphony kondrashin	lp: colosseum CRLP 172 lp: bruno 14021 cd: dante LYS 491-494 *dante edition suggests that the conductor is gauk*
stockholm 10-11 june 1953	stockholm festival orchestra ehrling	lp: columbia 33C 1036 lp: columbia (italy) QC 5025 lp: columbia (france) FC 1035/FCX 30245 lp: columbia (germany) WC 1036/C 70094/ C 91395 lp: hmv (spain) LBLP 1031 lp: angel 35315 lp: emi SLS 5004/HC 102 cd: testament SBT 1032
helsinki june 1954	finnish radio orchestra fougstedt	cd: ondine ODE 809

philadelphia
21-24
april
1959
	philadelphia
	orchestra
	ormandy
		lp: columbia (usa) ML 5492/MS 6157/Y-30489
		lp: philips ABL 3366/SABL 195/A01484L/
		    835 570AY
		lp: cbs 61041/60312
		lp: melodiya S10 22197-22198
		cd: sony MPK 44854/SB4K 76591/
		    SB3K 52516

moscow 1965	ussr state symphony rozhdestvensky	lp: melodiya D 016279-016280/S 01077-01078 lp: emi ASD 2407/2C069 94483/3C069 94483 lp: angel 40020 lp: eurodisc XGK 89515/XPK 88665 lp: chant du monde LDX 78649 lp: ricordi OCL 16264 cd: mobile fidelity MFCD 899 cd: vox CDX 5120 cd: zyx music 46109 cd: chant du monde LDC 278884 cd: rca/bmg 74321 341782/74321 407102 cd: melodiya SUCD 10 00479/CD10 00745/ CD10 00740 dvd video: emi classic archive DVB 599 6859 *excerpts* vhs video: warner/nvc arts 3984 230303 dvd video: warner/nvc arts 3984 230302

sibelius/**two humoresques for violin and orchestra**
moscow	ussr state	lp: melodiya D 016279-016280/S 01077-01078
1965	symphony	lp: emi ASD 2407/2C069 94483/3C065 94483
	rozhdesctevensky	lp: angel 40020
		lp: eurodisc XGK 89515/XPK 88665
		lp: chant du monde LDX 78649
		cd: chant du monde LDC 278884
		cd: vox CDX 5120
		cd: zyx music 46109
		cd: rca/bmg 74321 341782/74321 407102
		cd: melodiya SUCD10 00479/CD10 00745/ CD10 00740

BEDRICH SMETANA (1824-1884)
piano trio in g
moscow	oborin, piano	lp: melodiya D 028625-028626/D 3564-3565
1950	knushevitsky,	lp: monitor MC 2070
	cello	lp: eurodisc XK 79835
		lp: westminster XWN 18175
		cd: preiser 90595

LOUIS SPOHR (1784-1859)
duo in d for two violins
paris	i.oistrakh,	lp: melodiya D 14121-14122/S 0579-0580
march	second violin	lp: monitor MC 2058
1961		lp: concert hall SMSC 201
		lp: chant du monde LDX 8280
		cd: chant du monde LDC 278906
		cd: doremi DHR 7714
		cd: notablu 93.5107

IGOR STRAVINSKY (1882-1971)
violin concerto
paris	orchestre	lp: philips AL 3455/SAL 3455/A02315L/ 835 190AY/6585 003
1963	lamoureux	
	haitink	lp: philips (usa) PHM 500 050/PHS 900 050
		lp: melodiya D 013725-013726/S 0865-0866
		cd: philips 434 1672
		also issued by eterna
moscow	moscow	cd: revelation RV 10075
8 february	philharmonic	
1963	kondrashin	
berlin ddr	rundfunk-	lp: melodiya M10 46420-46421
8 march	sinfonie-orchester	cd: dante LYS 491-494
1965	sanderling	

JOSEF SUK (1874-1935)
love song op 7 no 1, arranged for violin and piano by kocian

moscow 1950	yampolsky, piano	78: melodiya 24409-24410 lp: melodiya D 028561-028562/D 10497-10498 lp: colosseum CRLP 105 lp: supraphon MKS 25007/LPM 237/ 　　DM 5222/SUEC 803 lp: parliament PLP 118 lp: monitor MC 2003 lp: eurodisc XAK 85315 cd: monitor MCD 72003
berlin ddr february 1954	n.walter, piano	lp: melodiya D 029743-029744/D 5028-5029 lp: eurodisc CKK 40442/ARK 16395
london 18-28 february 1956	yampolsky, piano	lp: columbia 33CX 1466/SAX 2253 lp: columbia (france) SAXF 149 lp: columbia (germany) WSX 604/SHZE 160 lp: angel 35354/60259 cd: testament 562 9142

three pieces for violin and piano, from op 17

moscow 1948	makarov, piano	lp: melodiya D 028561-028562 *this recording was not listed in world's encyclopedia of recorded music*

JOSEPH SZIGETI (1892-1973)
étude op 8 no 10 for violin and piano

date uncertain	diakov, piano	issued only in soviet union

KAROL SZYMANOWSKI (1883-1937)
violin concerto no 1

leningrad 1959	leningrad philharmonic sanderling	lp: melodiya D 05180-05181 lp: bruno 14043 lp: artia ALP 156 lp: eurodisc ZK 79843 cd: forlane UCD 16589 cd: urania (usa) US 5157 cd: chant du monde LDC 278941
warsaw 24 november 1961	warsaw philharmonic stryja	cd: preludio PHC 2149
berlin ddr 8 march 1965	rundfunk-sinfonie-orchester sanderling	cd: dante LYS 491-494

violin sonata no 1

stockholm june 1953	yampolsky, piano	lp: columbia 33CX 1201 lp: columbia (italy) QCX 10160 lp: columbia (france) FCX 355/FCX 30269 lp: columbia (germany) WCX 1201/C 90389 lp: hmv (spain) LALP 497 lp: angel 35163 lp: melodiya D 05180-05181 lp: colosseum CRLP 190 lp: bruno 14043 cd: testament SBT 1116 *also issued by vanguard*

fountains of arethusa, for violin and piano

moscow 1953	yampolsky, piano	lp: melodiya D 029743-029744/D 2163-2164 lp: supraphon LPM 237/DM 5552/ SUEC 803/MKS 25007 lp: parliament PLP 118 lp: bruno 14043 lp: monitor MC 2003 lp: monarch MWL 707 lp: concert hall MMS 2226 lp: chant du monde LDM 8175 cd: monitor MCD 72003

OTAR TAKTAKISHVILY (1924-1989)
concertino for violin and orchestra

moscow 1959	ussr state symphony taktakishvily	lp:	melodiya D 04944-04945/ S10 08017-08018

SERGEI TANEYEV (1856-1915)
suite de concert for violin and orchestra

london 24-25 february 1956	philharmonia malko	lp: lp: lp: lp: cd:	columbia 33CX 1390 angel 35355 melodiya D 021509-021510 emi SLS 5004 emi CDM 565 4192
date uncertain	ussr state symphony kondrashin	lp: lp:	bruno 14013 acropole APCC 60047

piano trio in d

moscow 1952	oborin, piano knushevitaky, cello	lp: lp: lp:	melodiya D 028545-028546/ D 10458-10459 monitor MC 2068 westminster XWN 18679

trio in d for two violins and viola

moscow 1950	bondarenko, second violin terian, viola	lp: lp:	melodiya D 028625-028626 monitor MC 2059 *this recording was not listed in world's encyclopedia of recorded music*

romance in a, arranged for violin and piano by feigin

moscow 27 october 1949	yampolsky, piano	78:	melodiya 17372-17373

GIUSEPPE TARTINI (1692-1770)
violin sonata in g minor "il trillo del diavolo"

moscow 1950	yampolsky, piano	78: melodiya 017901-017904 lp: melodiya D 508-509/D 5604-5605 lp: colosseum CRLP 148 lp: bruno 14019 lp: hall of fame HOF 524/HOFS 524 lp: musidisc RC 858 lp: period SPL 573 lp: dover HCR 5245 lp: chant du monde LDY 8068 cd: chant du monde LDC 278945
london 16-17 february 1956	yampolsky, piano	45: columbia (italy) ESBF 17119 lp: columbia 33CX 1415 lp: columbia (italy) QCX 10306 lp: columbia (france) FCX 654 lp: columbia (germany) WCX 1415/C 90529 lp: hmv (spain) LALP 475 lp: angel 35356 lp: melodiya D 028113-028114 lp: emi 1C147 52238-52239 cd: emi 562 9142 cd: testament SBT 1113
moscow 1970	bauer, piano	lp: melodiya SM 02931-02932 lp: angel 40197 lp: ricordi OCL 16231 lp: musical heritage society MHS 4551 cd: rca/bmg GD 69085 cd: zyx music 46038

violin sonata in g minor "didone abbandonata"

moscow 1970	bauer, piano	lp: melodiya SM 02931-02932 lp: angel 40197 lp: ricordi OCL 16231 lp: musical heritage society MHS 4551 cd: rca/bmg GD 69085 cd: zyx music 46038

tartini/**trio sonata in f for two violins and keyboard**

leipzig	i.oistrakh,	45: eterna 520 145
19 april	second violin	lp: dg LPM 18 393
1957	pischner,	lp: eterna 820 283
	harpsichord	lp: dg heliodor 89 561
		lp: decca (usa) DL 9950
		lp: heliodor (usa) H 25009/HS 25009
		cd: dg 473 5762
moscow	i.oistrakh,	lp: melodiya D 5670-5671/D 015349-015350
1959	second violin	lp: bruno 14019
	ginzburg, piano	lp: hall of fame HOF 516/HOFS 516

PIOTR TCHAIKOVSKY (1840-1893)
violin concerto

moscow	ussr large radio	78: melodiya 0651-0666
3-5	orchestra	78: supraphon B 40105-40109
february	gauk	78: ultraphon H 24077-24081
1938		78: compass (usa) C 201
		lp: melodiya D 03820-03821
		lp: colosseum CRLP 101
		lp: bruno 14016
		lp: period SHO 307/SPL 710/1153
		lp: hall of fame HOF 501/HOFS 501
		lp: musidisc RC 812
		lp: allegro royale ALL 1640
		lp: vox PL 516.160/GBY 16160
		lp: everest SDBR 3375
		lp: murray hill S-2760
		lp: chant du monde LDS 8167
		lp: trophy LP 9001
		lp: telefunken TW 30170
		lp: mk records DO 3820
		lp: eurodisc XKK 70185/ZK 77297/ XAK 87693
		cd: dante LYS 331-334
		cd: russian disc RDCD 15002
		cd: istituto discografico IDIS 6396
		cd: bastei BDGM 5
		cd: tuxedo TUXCD 1052

some editions named orchestra as bolshoi theatre orchestra and conductor as gauk or kondrashin

tchaikovsky/violin concerto/continued

dresden 10-11 february 1954	dresden staatskapelle konwitschny	lp: dg LPE 17 163/LPM 18 196/2726 087/ 2870 124 lp: dg heliodor 2700 111/89 668/478 437 lp: eterna LPM 1014/820 002 lp: supraphon DV 5410 lp: decca (usa) DL 9755/DX 141 lp: heliodor (usa) H 25071/HS 25071 cd: dg 423 3992/447 4272/459 3902 *89 668 incorrectly described orchestra as leipzig* *gewandhaus*
date uncertain	leningrad philharmonic mravinsky	cd: palladio PD 4200 *also issued by multisonic*
paris 1958	orchestre national dervaux	lp: melodiya D 14619-141620 *this issue may have named orchestra and conductor* *as moscow philharmonic and kondrashin*

philadelphia
14 december
1959
	philadelphia
	orchestra
	ormandy
		lp: columbia (usa) ML 5698/MS 6298/Y-30312
		lp: cbs BRG 72064/SBRG 72064/60312
		lp: supraphon 110 0217/SUA 10934/
		    SUAST 50934
		cd: sony MPK 44854/MY2K 46460/
		    SBK 46339

london 19 january 1960	royal philharmonic del mar	cd: bbc legends BBCL 41022
lisbon 27 june 1960	national orchestra of portugal freitas branco	cd: portugalsom SP 4084
turin 26 april 1963	rai torino orchestra kempe	cd: arkadia CDLSMH 34015/CDMP 415 cd: frequenz 041.011 cd: live classics best (japan) LCB 125 *arkadia editions suggest that this performance was in* *rome in 1960 with rai roma orchestra*

tchaikovsky/violin concerto/concluded
moscow	moscow	lp: melodiya D 024141-024142/S 01778-01779
27 september	philharmonic	lp: emi ASD 2918/2C069 97790/3C065 97790
1968	rozhdestvensky	lp: lp: chant du monde LDX 78419-78420
		lp: ricordi OCL 16213
		lp: supraphon 11 104221-5
		cd: chant du monde LDC 278884
		cd: rca/bmg 74321 341782/74321 407102
		cd: melodiya SUCD10 00239/CD10 00745/ CD10 00740
		dvd video: emi classic archive DVB 599 6859
		excerpts
		vhs video: warner/nvc arts 3984 230303
		dvd video: warner/nvc arts 3984 230302
dresden	dresden	unpublished video recording
22-23	staatskapelle	*ddr fernsehen*
april	siepuch	
1971		

filmed extracts from the concerto with oistrakh from 1937 (with piano) appears on warner/nvc arts vhs video 3984 230303 and dvd video 3984 230302

sérénade mélancolique pour violon et orchestre
moscow	ussr state	78: melodiya 12982-12985
1945	symphony	78: supraphon B 40002-40003
	kondrashin	78: compass (usa) C 202
		lp: colosseum CRLP 110
		cd: melodiya SUCD10 00239
		cd: doremi DHR 7742

tchaikovsky/**méditation from souvenir d'un lieu cher, for violin and piano**
warsaw   topilin, piano   78: syrena (poland) 8559
1935

moscow   yampolsky, piano   78: melodiya 393-394/5876-5877
1948   lp: melodiya D 6369-6370/D 016044-016045/
                                             D 022793-022794
                                         lp: colosseum CRLP 110
                                         lp: musidisc RC 858
                                         lp: vanguard VRS 6020
                                         lp: victor (japan) LS 2025
                                         cd: vanguard OVC 4080-4082
                                         cd: doremi DHR 7742
                                         cd: urania URN 22233

berlin ddr   n.walter, piano   lp: eterna LPM 1023/520 026
february   lp: saga FID 1005
1954

valse scherzo, arranged for violin and piano by besekirsky
moscow   yampolsky, piano   78: melodiya 393-394/9881-9882
1949   lp: melodiya D 6369-6370/D 16046-16047/
                                             D 022793-022794
                                         lp: colosseum CRLP 149
                                         lp: musidisc RC 858
                                         lp: chant du monde LDA 8075
                                         lp: vanguard VRS 6020
                                         lp: concert hall MMS 2226
                                         lp: eurodisc CK 40446
                                         cd: chant du monde LDC 278945
                                         cd: vanguard OVC 4080-4082
                                         cd: doremi DHR 7742

berlin ddr   yampolsky, piano   lp: melodoya M10 46361-46362
7 april
1952

london   yampolsky, piano   45: columbia SEL 1577/ESL 6252
18-28   45: columbia (italy) SEBQ 219/ESLQ 1007
february   lp: columbia 33CX 1466/SAX 2253
1956   lp: columbia (france) SAXF 149
                                         lp: columbia (germany) WSX 604/SHZE 160
                                         lp: angel 35354/60259
                                         cd: testament SBT 1115
                                         cd: disky DC 703512
                                         cd: emi 762 9142

tchaikovsky/**piano trio in a minor**
moscow	igumnov, piano	lp: melodiya S10 05526-05527
1939	knushevitsky, cello	*first movement only; this recording was not listed in world's encyclopedia of recorded music*

moscow	oborin, piano	78: melodiya 015696-015707
march	knushevitsky,	78: supraphon H 24125-24130
1948	cello	cd: doremi DHR 7742
		cd: leningrad masters LM 1307
		leningrad masters edition is dated 1961

string quartet no 1
moscow	bondarenko,	78: melodiya 295-298/019779-019786
1950	second violin	lp: melodiya D 4180-4181/D 022793-022794
	terian, viola	lp: colosseum CRLP 190
	knushevitsky,	cd: doremi DHR 7701
	cello	*andante cantabile only*
		78: melodiya 1054-1055/018266-018267

PEARL TOWNSEND (born 1886)
berceuse for violin and piano
warsaw	unnamed	78: syrena (poland) 8600
1935	pianist	

MOISHEI VAINBERG (1919-1996)
rhapsody on moldavian themes, arranged for violin and piano
moscow	vainberg, piano	lp: melodiya D 05622-05623
1952		lp: classic editions (usa) CE 3002
		lp: colosseum CRLP 011

HENRI VIEUXTEMPS (1820-1881)
souvenir op 20 no 4 for violin and piano
date uncertain	yampolsky, piano	78: melodiya 19537-19538

vieuxtemps/**two romances for violin and piano**

date uncertain	yampolsky, violin	lp: melodiya D 028807-028808/D 5028-5029 lp: bruno 14018 lp: hall of fame HOF 519/HOFS 519 lp: musidisc RC 858 lp: decca (usa) DL 9882 lp: concert hall MMS 2226 lp: chant du monde LDA 8175/LDXSP 1801 cd: chant du monde LDC 278945 *this recording was not listed in world's encyclopedia of recorded music*

GIOVANNI BATTISTA VIOTTI (1755-1824)
violin concerto no 22

moscow 1948	ussr state symphony kondrashin	lp: melodiya D 026211-026212 lp: eurodisc XAK 85315/XGK 89410/ XPK 88665 cd: rca/bmg GD 69085 *this recording was not listed in world's encyclopedia of recorded music*

TOMMASO VITALI (1663-1745)
chaconne in g minor, arranged for violin and piano by charlier

moscow 1950	yampolsky, piano	lp: melodiya D 028113-028114 lp: hall of fame HOF 519/HOFS 519 lp: monitor MC 2042 cd: monitor MCD 72009 cd: rca/bmg 74321 431802/74321 407102 cd: melodiya CD10 00745/CD10 00742 *this recording was not listed in world's encyclopedia of recorded music*
berlin ddr 7 april 1952	yampolsky, piano	lp: melodiya D 007529-007530/ M10 46361-46362

ANTONIO VIVALDI (1675-1741)
concerto in c for two violins and strings rv509

philadelphia 31 december 1959	philadelphis orchestra ormandy stern, second violin	45: philips 494 100EE lp: columbia (usa) ML 5604/MS 6204 lp: philips fontana CFL 1070/SCFL 136/ 699 061CL/876 008CY lp: supraphon SUA 10932/SUAST 50932 lp: cbs BRG 72082/SBRG 72082 cd: sony SM2K 66472

concerto in d for two violins and strings rv512

philadelphia 31 december 1959	philadelphia orchestra ormandy stern, second violin	lp: columbia (usa) ML 5604/MS 6204 lp: philips fontana CFL 1070/SCFL 136/ 699 061CL/876 008CY lp: supraphon SUA 10932/SUAST 50932 lp: cbs BRG 72082/SBRG 72082 cd: sony SM2K 66472

concerto in d for two violins and strings rv514

philadelphia 31 december 1959	philadelphia orchestra ormandy stern, second violin	lp: columbia (usa) ML 5604/MS 6204 lp: philips fontana CFL 1070/SCFL 136/ 699 061CL/876 008CY lp: supraphon SUA 10932/SUAST 50932 lp: cbs BRG 72082/SBRG 72082 cd: sony SM2K 66472
london 26 february 1961	london philharmonic sargent i.oistrakh, second violin	unpublished radio broadcast *bbc london*
moscow 17 may 1961	moscow philharmonic kondrashin i.oistrakh, second violin	cd: revelation RV 10039 cd: yedang classics CT 10031
warsaw 24 november 1961	warsaw philharmonic stryja i.oistrakh, second violin	cd: preludio PHC 2149

vivaldi/**concerto in g for two violins and strings rv517**

philadelphia	philadelphia	lp: columbia (usa) ML 5604/MS 6204
31 december	orchestra	lp: philips fontana CFL 1070/SCFL 136/
1959	ormandy	699 061CL/876 008CY
	stern,	lp: supraphon SUA 10932/SUAST 50932
	second violin	lp: cbs BRG 72082/SBRG 72082
		cd: sony SM2K 66472

concerto in a for two violins and strings rv522

philadelphia	philadelphia	45: philips ABE 10181/409 020AE
24 december	orchestra	lp: columbia (usa) ML 5087/M4K 42003/
1955	ormandy	MG 33328
	stern,	lp: philips ABL 3138/A01239L/G05650R
	second violin	lp: melodiya M10 46429-46430
		lp: eterna 825 612
		cd: sony SM3K 45952/SM2K 66472

leipzig	gewandhaus-	lp: dg LPE 17 160/LPM 18 393
april	orchester	lp: eterna 720 031
1957	konwitschny	lp: decca (usa) DL 9950
	i.oistrakh,	lp: bruno 14109
	second violin	cd: berlin classics BC 21302/BC 01272

walthamstow	royal	lp: dg LPM 18 714/SLPM 138 714/2535 067
march	philharmonic	lp: eterna 720 162/825 882
1961	goossens	lp: melodiya D 8267-8268/S 157-158
	i.oistrakh,	lp: electrecord STECE 0889
	second violin	cd: dg 419 8552/463 6162

concerto in f for three violins and strings rv551

london	moscow	cd: bbc music magazine MM 99
28 september	philharmonic	
1963	kondrashin	
	menuhin,	
	second violin	
	i.oistrakh,	
	third violin	

PANCHO VLADIGEROV (born 1899)
fantasy on a bulgarian dance theme for violin and piano
moscow	yampolsky, piano	lp: melodiya D 028113-028114/D 6369-6370
1951		lp: supraphon LPM 237/DM 5222/ MKS 25007
		lp: parliament PLP 118
		lp: colosseum CRLP 153
		lp: classic edition (usa) CE 3002

vardar, arranged for violin and piano
also known as bulgarian rhapsody
moscow	yampolsky, piano	78: melodiya 19026-19028
1951		lp: melodiya D 6369-6370

RICHARD WAGNER (1813-1883)
albumblatt, arranged for violin and piano by wilhelmi
moscow	yampolsky, piano	lp: melodiya D 5028-5029
1950		lp: monitor MC 2003
		cd: monitor MCD 72003
		this recording was not listed in world's encyclopedia of recorded music
tokyo 7-8 march 1955	yampolsky, piano	lp: victor (japan) LS 2026

HENRYK WIENIAWSKI (1835-1880)
scherzo tarantelle for violin and piano
date uncertain	yampolsky, piano	lp: melodiya D 022227-022228

étude in e for violin and piano
date uncertain	yampolsky, piano	78: melodiya 2163-2164
		lp: melodiya D 029743-029744
		lp: decca (usa) DL 9882

wieniawski/étude caprice no 2 for two violins
leipzig	i.oistrakh,	45: dg EPL 30 286
19 april	second violin	45: eterna 520 119
1957		lp: eterna 720 048
		lp: dg heliodor 89 688/478 437/2870 124
		lp: decca (usa) DL 9962
		cd: dg 459 0162/459 0672

étude caprice no 3 for two violins
moscow	i.oistrakh,	cd: revelation RV 10039
21 may	second violin	cd: yedang classics CT 10031
1954		

étude caprice no 4 for two violins
leipzig	i.oistrakh,	45: dg EPL 30 286
19 april	second violin	45: eterna 520 119
1957		lp: eterna 720 048
		lp: dg heliodor 89 688/478 437/2870 124
		lp: decca (usa) DL 9962
		cd: dg 459 0162/459 0672/463 6162

étude caprice no 5 for two violins
leipzig	i.oistrakh,	45: dg EPL 30 286
19 april	second violin	45: eterna 520 119
1957		lp: eterna 720 048
		lp: dg heliodor 89 688/478 437/2870 124
		lp: decca (usa) DL 9962
		cd: dg 459 0162/459 0672

légende for violin and piano
moscow	yampolsky, piano	78: melodiya 2163-2164
1952		lp: melodiya D 029743-029744
		lp: colosseum CRLP 251
		lp: decca (usa) DL 9882
		lp: monarch MWL 707
		lp: concert hall MMS 2226
		lp: chant du monde LDA 8175/LDX 8360
		cd: chant du monde LDC 278943
london	yampolsky, piano	lp: columbia 33CX 1466/SAX 2253
18-26		lp: columbia (france) SAXF 149
february		lp: columbia (germany) WSX 604/SHZE 160
1956		lp: angel 35354/60259
		cd: disky DC 703512
		cd: emi CDM 769 3672/762 9142

HUGO WOLF (1860-1903)
verborgenheit, arranged for violin and piano

warsaw 1935	topilin, piano	78: syrena (poland) 8601

EUGENE YSAYE (1858-1931)
amitié, for two violins and orchestra

london 26 february 1961	london philharmonic sargent i.oistrakh, second violin	unpublished radio broadcast *bbc london*
moscow 17 may 1961	moscow philharmonic kondrashin i.oistrakh, second violin	cd: revelation RV 10039 cd: yedang classics CT 10031
london august 1969	ussr state symphony svetlanov i.oistrakh, second violin	cd: bbc legends BBCL 40602

solo violin sonata no 3

moscow 1950	78: supraphon 18900 78: ultraphon E 23327 lp: colosseum CRLP 150 lp: parlophone PMA 1175 lp: eurodisc EK 70600 lp: vanguard VRS 6024 cd: vanguard OVC 4080-4082
paris 1966	lp: philips SAL 3589/802 707AY/6570 206 lp: philips (usa) PHM 500 112/PHS 900 112 lp: melodiya D 020403-020404/ S 01527-01528 lp: chant du monde LDX 78362 cd: chant du monde LDC 278944 cd: philips 420 7772

ysaye/**extase for violin and piano**
london	yampolsky, piano	lp: columbia 33CX 1466/SAX 2253
18-27		lp: columbia (france) SAXF 149
february		lp: columbia (germany) WSX 604/SHZE 160
1956		lp: angel 35354/60259
		lp: capitol ZST 44001
		cd: emi CDM 769 3672/762 9142

poeme élégaique for violin and piano
moscow	yampolsky, piano	lp: melodiya D 028807-028808/D 5028-5029
1951		lp: bruno 14018
		lp: decca (usa) DL 9882
		lp: eurodisc XRK 27315
		lp: fondation ysaye FEY 3001

ALEXANDER ZARZYCKI (1834-1895)
mazurka for violin and piano
moscow	yampolsky, piano	lp: melodiya D 04044-04045
1952		lp: bruno 32002
		lp: monitor MC 2003
		lp: concert hall MMS 2226
		lp: chant du monde LDA 8175
		cd: chant du monde LDC 278945
		cd: monitor MCD 72003
		this recording was not listed in world's encyclopedia of recorded music

london	yampolsky, piano	lp: columbia 33CX 1466/SAX 2253
18-28		lp: columbia (france) SAXF 149
february		lp: columbia (germany) WSX 604/SHZE 160
1956		lp: angel 35354/60259
		cd: testament SBT 1116
		cd: emi 762 9142

Concertgebouw, Amsterdam
Zondag 25 April 1937 te 2.30

Middagconcert

(onder auspiciën van de A.V.R.O.)

het Concertgebouw-orkest

onder leiding van

Eduard van Beinum

N. Rimsky-Korsakoff Shéhérazade, d'après ,,Mille et une
1844—1908 nuits", Suite symphonique (op. 35)

    I. La mer et le vaisseau de Sindbad
    II. Le récit du Prince Kalender
    III. Le jeune prince et la jeune princesse
    IV. Fête à Bagdad. La mer. Le vaisseau se brise contre un rocher surmonté d'un guerrier d'arrain. Conclusion

P. I. Tschaikowsky Concert D gr. t. (op. 35)
1840—1893 voor viool en orkest

Allegro
Canzonetta
Finale: Allegro vivacissimo

solist: David Oistrakh

david oistrakh
as conductor

this listing does not include recordings in which oistrakh directs from the violin: those are to be found in the main discography

JOHANN SEBASTIAN BACH (1685-1750)
orchestral suite no 2

moscow	moscow	lp: melodiya SM 03343-03344
1972	philharmonic	lp: chant du monde LDX 78564
		cd: zyx music 46114

concerto for two violins bwv1043

date	bolshoi theatre	lp: melodiya D 011075-011076/S 0439-0430
uncertain	orchestra	*this is probably an arrangement of the concerto for string orchestra*

BELA BARTOK (1881-1945)
concerto for orchestra

moscow	moscow	cd: revelation RV 10015
25 february	philharmonic	
1972		

LUDWIG VAN BEETHOVEN (1770-1827)
symphony no 4

berlin ddr	rundfunk-	lp: melodiya M10 4619-4620
19 april	sinfonie-orchester	cd: revelation RV 10079
1971		

violin concerto

london	moscow	cd: bbc legends BBCL 40192
28 september	philharmonic	
1963	menuhin, violin	

vienna	vienna symphony	lp: melodiya SM 03011-03012
may	i.oistrakh, violin	lp: eterna 827 355
1970		lp: eurodisc XHK 25932/XFK 88458
		lp: rca/bmg GL 25005

egmont overture

moscow	moscow	lp: melodiya SM 05365-05366
1970	philharmonic	

HECTOR BERLIOZ (1803-1869)
harold en italie

moscow 1964	moscow philharmonic barshai, viola	lp: melodiya D 014717-014718/S 0893-0894 lp: angel 40001 lp: chant du monde LDX 78369 cd: melodiya SUCD10 00484
moscow 28 march 1972	ussr state symphony tolypygo, viola	cd: revelation RV 10051
vienna 8 june 1972	vienna symphony i.oistrakh, viola	lp: melodiya S10 35415-35416

JOHANNES BRAHMS (1833-1897)
symphony no 1

moscow 14 october 1968	moscow philharmonic	cd: revelation RV 10072
prague 15 may 1972	czech philharmonic	lp: melodiya M10 46419-46420

symphony no 2

dresden 11 october 1963	dresden staatskapelle	lp: melodiya M10 46361-46362
moscow 20 december 1968	ussr state symphony	cd: revelation RV 10072
moscow 6 october 1974	moscow philharmonic	lp: melodiya S10 06643-06644

MAX BRUCH (1838-1920)
violin concerto no 1

walthamstow	royal	lp: dg LPE 17 230/SLPE 133 230/135 039/
february	philharmonic	2535 176
1961	i.oistrakh, violin	lp: melodiya D 08285-08286/SM 0155-0156

ARCANGELO CORELLI (1653-1713)
concerti grossi op 6, complete set of 12 concertos

date	moscow	lp: eurodisc XFK 28662
uncertain	philharmonic	
	i.oistrakh, violin	

concerti grossi op 6, concertos 1-4 only

date	moscow	lp: melodiya S10 05919-05920
uncertain	philharmonic	cd: zyx music 46029
	soloists	cd: icone 9413

ANTONIN DVORAK (1841-1904)
violin concerto

date	moscow	lp: melodiya SM 1903-1904
uncertain	philharmonic	lp: angel 40185
	pikaizen, violin	lp: chant du monde LDX 78441

EDVARD GRIEG (1843-1907)
piano concerto

moscow	ussr state	cd: revelation RV 10050
12 november	symphony	*a date of 12 november 1972 is also mentioned for this*
1967	richter, piano	*performance, but neither the 1967 nor 1972 dates*
		appear in the list of richter's public concerts
bergen	bergen symphony	lp: MR 46/MJA 1973/JJA 1972
5 june	richter, piano	cd: intaglio INCD 7511
1968		

EDOUARD LALO (1823-1892)
symphonie espagnole pour violon et orchestre

date	ussr state	lp: melodiya D 012355-012356/S 0649-0650
uncertain	symphony	lp: eterna 826 213
	i.oistrakh, violin	lp: eurodisc XAK 86039
		also issued by chant du monde

GUSTAV MAHLER (1860-1911)
symphony no 4

date	moscow	lp: melodiya D 021039-021040/
uncertain	philharmonic	S 01583-01584
	vishnevskaya	lp: angel 40076
		cd: revelation RV 10078
		also issued by chant du monde

ALESSANDRO MARCELLO (1669-1747)
oboe concerto in d

date	moscow	lp: melodiya D 024359-024360/
uncertain	philharmonic	SM 01905-01906
	soloists	lp: chant du monde LDXA 78488
	trubashnik, oboe	

FELIX MENDELSSOHN-BARTHOLDY (1809-1847)
violin concerto

moscow	moscow	cd: revelation RV 10022
22 january	philharmonic	
1967	parchomenko,	
	violin	

WOLFGANG AMADEUS MOZART (1756-1791)
symphony no 41 "jupiter"

vienna	vienna	cd: andante 4994
28 may	philharmonic	
1972		

serenade no 13 "eine kleine nachtmusik"

date	moscow	cd: revelation RV 10022
uncertain	philharmonic	
salzburg	vienna	cd: orfeo C302 921B
23 august	philharmonic	
1972		

mozart/**divertimento no 11 k251**
date	moscow	lp: melodiya D 024359-024360/
uncertain	philharmonic	SM 01905-01906

piano concerto no 20 k466
date	ussr state	lp: melodiya D 11733-11734/S 571-572
uncertain	symphony	
	devetzi, piano	

violin concerto no 1 k207
date	moscow	lp: melodiya SM 03307-03308
uncertain	philharmonic	lp: chant du monde LDX 78579
	kagan, violin	

violin concerto no 3 k216
moscow	moscow	lp: melodiya SM 01917-01918
25 february	philharmonic	lp: chant du monde LDX 78455
1970	kagan, violin	

violin concerto no 4 k218
date	moscow	lp: melodiya D 024847-024848/
uncertain	philharmonic	SM 02295-02296
	fain, violin	

date	moscow	lp: melodiya SM 03307-03308
uncerrain	philharmonic	lp: chant du monde LDX 83579
	kagan, violin	

violin concerto no 5 k219
moscow	moscow	lp: melodiya SM 01917-01919
25 february	philharmonic	cd: icone 9405
1970	kagan, violin	

mozart/**violin concerto no 6 k268**
moscow	moscow	lp: melodiya SM 02765-02766
5 april	philharmonic	cd: icone 9405
1971	fichtenholtz, violin	

adagio for violin and orchestra k261
moscow	moscow	lp: melodiya SM 02765-02766
5 april	philharmonic	
1971	fichtenholtz, violin	

rondo for violin and orchestra k373
moscow	moscow	lp: melodiya SM 02295-02296
1969	philharmonic fain, violin	

moscow	moscow	lp: melodiya SM 02765-02766
5 april	philharmonic	
1971	fichtenholtz, violin	

GIOVANNI BATTISTA PERGOLESI (1710-1736)
concertino in b flat, arranged by dushkin
moscow	moscow	lp: melodiya D 024847-024848/
1969	philharmonic fain, violin	SM 02295-02296

SERGE PROKOFIEV (1891-1953)
symphony no 5
moscow	moscow	lp: melodiya D 017507-017508/
6 march	philharmonic	S 01237-01238/M10 46419 000
1967		lp: angel 40003
		also issued by chant du monde

piano concerto no 1
moscow	ussr state	cd: russian disc RDCD 16301
1971	symphony lubimov, piano	

romeo and juliet, 5 scenes from the ballet
prague	czech	lp: melodiya M10 46419 000
20 may	philharmonic	cd: supraphon SU 216 2011
1972		

FRANZ SCHUBERT (1797-1828)
symphony no 2

date uncertain	moscow philharmonic	cd: revelation RV 10022
berlin ddr date uncertain	rundfunk-sinfonie orchester	unpublished radio broadcast *kulturradio berlin*

ROBERT SCHUMANN (1810-1856)
cello concerto

moscow 1969	ussr state symphony rostropovich, cello	cd: russian disc RDCD 11106

manfred overture

moscow 1970	moscow philharmonic	lp: melodiya 05365-05366

DIMITRI SHOSTAKOVICH (1906-1975)
symphony no 7 "leningrad"

moscow 1972	ussr state symphony	lp: melodiya D 033449-033452

symphony no 9

moscow 29 december 1969	ussr state symphony	cd: russian disc RDCD 11192

cello concerto no 1

moscow 24 january 1965	moscow philharmonic rostropovich, cello	cd: revelation RV 10087 cd: russian disc RDCD 11106

cello concerto no 2

moscow 12 november 1967	moscow philharmonic rostropovich, cello	cd: revelation RV 10087

JEAN SIBELIUS (1865-1957)
violin concerto

budapest	hungarian state	vhs video: warner/nvc arts 3984 230303
1972	orchestra	dvd video: warner/nvc arts 3984 230302
	kremer, violin	*rehearsal extract only*

RICHARD STRAUSS (1864-1949)
till eulenspiegels lustige streiche

moscow	ussr state	cd: revelation RV 10026
28 february	symphony	cd: yedang classics CT 10023
1966		

PIOTR TCHAIKOVSKY (1840-1893)
symphony no 5

salzburg	vienna	cd: orfeo C302 921B
23 august	philharmonic	
1972		

symphony no 6 "pathétique"

moscow	ussr state	lp: melodiya D 024139-024140/
28-29	symphony	SM 01781-01782
september		lp: chant du monde LDX 78419
1968		cd: revelation RV 10050

violin concerto

date	moscow	lp: melodiya 017433-017434/
uncertain	philharmonic	S 01243-01244
	i.oistrakh, violin	lp: angel 40009
		also issued by eterna and chant du monde
prague	czech	cd: supraphon SU 216 2011
20 may	philharmonic	*filmed extract from the performance on warner/ nvc arts*
1972	hudecek, violin	*vhs video 3984 230303 and dvd video 3984302*

variations on a rococo theme for cello and orchestra

date	moscow	cd: revelation RV 10077
uncertain	philharmonic	

ANTONIO VIVALDI (1678-1741)
flute concerto in g "la notte"
date	moscow	lp: melodiya D 024359-024360/
uncertain	philharmonic	SM 01905-01906
	hoffmann, flute	lp: chant du monde LDX 78488

EUGENE YSAYE (1858-1931)
mazurka in b for violin and orchestra
date	moscow	lp: melodiya D 023101-023102/
uncertain	philharmonic	SM 01903-01904
	pikaizen, violin	*also issued by chant du monde*

wolfgang schneiderhan
1915-2002
the discography

ALFREDO D'AMBROSIO
serenade for violin and piano

vienna	schulhof, piano	78: columbia DX 477
1934		78: columbia (usa) 5124M
		cd: amadeo 431 3442/431 3432

JOHANN SEBASTIAN BACH (1685-1750)
violin concerto no 1 bwv1041

vienna	vienna	lp: private issue P 1017
1 july	philharmonic	cd: music and arts CD 897
1944	knappertsbusch	cd: tahra TAH 320-322
		cd: archipel ARPCD 0102
		also issued by seven seas in japan
zürich	collegium	78: dg archiv AVM 2462
4 november	musicum	45: dg archiv EPA 37 025
1953	sacher	
lucerne	lucerne festival	lp: dg archiv APM 14 086
28-29	strings	lp: decca (usa) ARC 3099
january	baumgartner	lp: contour classics 2870 126
1957		cd: dg original masters 477 5263
vienna	vienna baroque	lp: concert hall SMSA 2552
1967	orchestra	
	atzmon	

violin concerto no 2 bwv1042

lucerne	lucerne festival	lp: dg LPM 18 460
8-10	orchestra	lp: dg archiv APM 14 086
december	baumgartner	lp: decca (usa) ARC 3099
1956		lp: contour classics 2870 126
		cd: dg original masters 477 5263
vienna	vienna baroque	lp: concert hall SMSA 2552
1967	orchestra	
	atzmon	

bach/**concerto for two violins bwv1043**
lucerne	lucerne festival	lp: dg archiv APM 14 086
12 december	strings	lp: decca (usa) ARC 3099
1956	baumgartner,	lp: contour classics 2870 126
	conductor and	cd: dg original masters 477 5263
	second violin	

brandenburg concerto no 5
vienna	vienna	lp: french furtwängler society SWF 8401-8402
21-22	philharmonic	lp: refrain (japan) AT 13-14
december	niedermayer, flute	
1940	furtwängler,	
	conductor	
	and piano	

solo violin partita no 2 bwv1004
vienna	lp: dg archiv AP 13 029
12-15	*chaconne only*
january	45: dg archiv EPA 37 051
1955	lp: heliodor (usa) H 25030/HS 25030

chaconne from solo violin partita no 2
vienna	columbia unpublished
6 october	*recording incomplete*
1947	

vienna	78: columbia (austria) LVX 41-42
14 october	cd: opus kura (japan) OPK 2020
1947	

sonata no 1 for violin and keyboard bwv1014
vienna	k.richter,	lp: dg archiv SAPM 198 381-198 382/
21-27	harpsichord	2708 011
february		
1966		

sonata no 2 for violin and keyboard bwv1015
schwetzingen	seemann, piano	cd: orfeo C473 971B
15 june		
1964		

vienna	k.richter,	lp: dg archiv SAPM 198 381-198 382/
21-27	harpsichord	SAPM 199 008/2708 011
february		
1966		

bach/**sonata no 3 for violin and keyboard bwv1016**
vienna   k.richter,   lp: dg archiv SAPM 198 381-198 382/
21-27   harpsichord   2708 011
february
1966

sonata no 4 for violin and keyboard bwv1017
vienna   k.richter,   lp: dg archiv SAPM 198 381-198 382/
21-27   harpsichord   2708 011
february
1966

largo siciliana from sonata no 4
vienna   wührer, piano   columbia unpublished
11 december
1947

sonata no 5 for violin and keyboard bwv1018
vienna   k.richter,   lp: dg archiv SAPM 198 381-198 382/
21-27   harpsichord   2708 011
february
1966

sonata no 6 for violin and keyboard bwv1019
vienna   k.richter,   lp: dg archiv SAPM 198 381-198 382/
21-27   harpsichord   2708 011
february
1966

bach/**cantata no 202** "weichet nur betrübte schatten"
salzburg	lucerne festival	lp: dg LPM 18 606/SLPM 138 086
3 august	strings	
1959	baumgartner	
	seefried	

meinem hirten bleib ich treu, aria from cantata no 92
vienna	legge, organ	lp: emi EX 29 10563/EX 29 12363
24 october	seefried	*unpublished columbia 78rpm recording*
1946		

genügsamkeit ist ein schatz, aria from cantata no 144
vienna	legge, organ	columbia unpublished
24 october	seefried	
1946		

BELA BARTOK (1881-1945)
violin sonata no 2
vienna	seemann, piano	lp: dg LPM 18 400
7-8		lp: decca (usa) DL 9980
april		
1957		

rumanian folkdances, arranged for violin and piano by szekely
salzburg	hirsch, piano	45: dg EPL 30 334
29-30		
july		
1957		

LUDWIG VAN BEETHOVEN (1770-1827)
violin concerto

munich 4 may 1949	munich philharmonic knappertsbusch	unpublished radio broadcast *bayerischer rundfunk*
berlin 17-21 may 1953	berlin philharmonic van kempen	78: dg LVM 72366-72368 lp: dg LPM 18 099 lp: decca (usa) DL 9784 lp: eterna 820 005 cd: dg original masters 477 5263
berlin 18 may 1953	berlin philharmonic furtwängler	lp: dg LPM 18 855/KL 27-31 lp: dg heliodor 88 024/2535 809/2730 005 cd: dg amadeo 431 3452/431 3432 cd: dg original masters 474 7282/477 5030 cd: japanese furtwängler society WFJ 33-34
rome 30 january 1954	rai roma orchestra celibidache	lp: melodram MEL 201
cologne 18 november 1954	wdr orchestra sawallisch	unpublished radio broadcast *westdeutscher rundfunk*
salzburg 24 august 1955	vienna philharmonic kubelik	unpublished radio broadcast *österreichischer rundfunk*
berlin 29-30 april 1959	berlin philharmonic jochum	lp: dg SLPM 138 045
berlin 17-20 may 1962	berlin philharmonic jochum	lp: dg LPM 18 824/SLPM 138 824/ 138 999/2535 120 cd: dg 413 1452 cd: dg originals 447 4032 *this performance uses cadenzas written by beethoven* *for the piano version of the concerto*

beethoven/**triple concerto**
berlin	rso berlin	lp: dg LPEM 19 236/SLPEM 136 236/
30 may-	fricsay	2535 153/2721 128/2726 008
1 june	anda, piano	cd: dg 429 9342/439 7372/477 5263
1960	fournier, cello	

violin romance no 1
munich	bayerisches	lp: emi SHZE 281
1-10	staatsorchester	
october	heger	
1969		

violin romance no 2
munich	bayerisches	lp: emi SHZE 281
1-10	staatsorchester	
october	heger	
1969		

violin sonata op 12 no 1
vienna	kempff, piano	lp: dg LPM 18 083
september		cd: dg originals 463 6052
1952		

vienna	seemann, piano	lp: dg LPM 18 621/SLPM 138 621
11-13		
may		
1959		

violin sonata op 12 no 2
vienna	kempff, piano	lp: dg LPM 18 083
september		cd: dg originals 463 6052
1952		

vienna	seemann, piano	lp: dg LPM 18 621/SLPM 138 621
18-19		
may		
1959		

beethoven/**violin sonata op 12 no 3**

vienna september 1952	kempff, piano	lp: dg LPM 18 138 cd: dg originals 463 6052
vienna 14-15 may 1959	seemann, piano	lp: dg LPM 18 622/SLPM 138 622
schwetzingen 15 june 1964	seemann, piano	cd: orfeo C473 971B

violin sonata op 23

vienna september 1952	kempff, piano	lp: dg LPM 18 138 cd: dg originals 463 6052
vienna 13-14 may 1959	seemann, piano	lp: dg LPM 18 622/SLPM 138 622

violin sonata op 24 "spring"

vienna 23-25 november 1947	wührer, piano	columbia unpublished *recording incomplete*
vienna september 1952	kempff, piano	78: dg LVM 72 312-72 313 lp: dg LPM 18 082/LPE 17 164 cd: dg originals 463 6052
vienna 27-28 may 1959	seemann, piano	lp: dg LPM 18 620/SLPM 138 128/ 135 148/2535 321 cd: dg 453 8042

beethoven/**violin sonata op 30 no 1**
vienna september 1952	kempff, piano	lp: dg LPM 18 082 cd: dg originals 463 6052
vienna 24-25 may 1959	seemann, piano	lp: dg LPM 18 622/SLPM 138 122

violin sonata op 30 no 2
vienna 1 december 1947	wührer, piano	78: columbia LX 1190-1193/LX 8673-8676 lp: melodiya M10 46983 006 cd: partita (japan) PC 9207-9208 *recording completed on 6 december 1947; melodiya edition incorrectly dated 1942*
vienna september 1952	kempff, piano	78: dg LVM 72 353-72 354 lp: dg LPM 18 209 cd: dg originals 463 6052
vienna 23-24 may 1959	seemann, piano	lp: dg LPM 18 623/SLPM 138 123

violin sonata op 30 no 3
vienna september 1952	kempff, piano	lp: dg LPM 18 144 cd: dg originals 463 6052
vienna 16-17 may 1959	seemann, piano	lp: dg LPM 18 621/SLPM 138 121

beethoven/**violin sonata op 47 "kreutzer"**
vienna	kempff, piano	lp: dg LPM 18 092
september		cd: dg 459 0142
1952		cd: dg originals 463 6052

vienna	seemann, piano	lp: dg LPM 18 620/SLPM 138 120/
15-18		135 148/2535 321
may		cd: dg 445 4792
1959		

violin sonata op 96
vienna	kempff, piano	78: dg LVM 72 376-72 377
september		lp: dg LPM 18 209
1952		cd: dg 459 0142
		cd: dg originals 463 6052

vienna	seemann, piano	lp: dg LPM 18 623/SLPM 138 123
19-21		
may		
1959		

piano trio no 5 "ghost"
salzburg	fischer, piano	lp: discocorp BWS 735
8 august	mainardi, cello	lp: cetra DOC 35
1953		cd: arkadia CD 569/CDHP 568
		cd: orfeo C593 021B
		sender rot-weiss-rot

piano trio no 6 "archduke"
salzburg	fischer, piano	lp: discocorp BWS 735
9 august	mainardi, cello	lp: cetra LO 518
1952		cd: orfeo C593 021B
		sender rot-weiss-rot

beethoven/**string quartet op 18 no 6**
vienna   strasser,   cd: orfeo C402 951B
1949-1950   second violin
                   moravec, viola
                   krotschak, cello

string quartet op 59 no 1 "rasumovsky"
vienna   strasser,   cd: orfeo C315 931B
september   second violin   *reichsrundfunk recording; also issued in japan*
1944   moravec, viola   *by madrigal*
                   krotschak, cello

string quartet op 95
vienna   strasser,   78: columbia LX 8727-8728
22-24   second violin   78: columbia (france) LFX 933-934
february   moravec, viola   *recording completed on 7 march 1949*
1949   krotschak, cello

string quartet op 131
vienna   strasser,   cd: orfeo C315 931B
september   second violin   *reichsrundfunk recording*
1944   moravec, viola
                   krotschak, cello

JOHANNES BRAHMS (1833-1897)
violin concerto
dresden   dresden   78: columbia (germany) LWX 331-335
january   staatskapelle   lp: emi 1C137 53505-53507M
1940   böhm   cd: toshiba SGR 1205-1208
                                          cd: opus kura OPK 2020
                                          cd: urania URN 22149

berlin   berlin   lp: dg LPM 18 132
22 may   philharmonic   lp: dg heliodor 89 519
1953   van kempen   cd: dg original masters 477 5263

cologne   wdr orchestra   unpublished radio broadcast
14 november   dohnanyi   *westdeutscher rundfunk*
1960

brahms/**double concerto**

lucerne 24 august 1949	lucerne festival orchestra furtwängler mainardi, cello	lp: japanese furtwängler society W 19 cd: as-disc AS 372 cd: urania URN 22114 cd: music and arts CD 1018 cd: japanese furtwängler centre WDHC 003
salzburg 12 august 1956	vienna philharmonic böhm mainardi, cello	cd: refrain (japan) DR 92 0039 cd: orfeo C359 941A *both issues incorrectly dated 1957*

berlin
3-5
june
1961
	rso berlin
	fricsay
	starker, cello
		lp: dg LPM 18 753/LPE 17 237/39 126/
		   SLPM 138 753/SLPE 133 237/
		   139 126/2535 140/2726 008
		cd: dg 429 9342/439 7372

cologne 18 september 1964	wdr orchestra dohnanyi fournier, cello	unpublished radio broadcasr *westdeutscher rundfunk*

violin sonata no 1

vienna 10-11 january 1952	wührer, piano	78: dg LVM 72 175-72 176 lp: dg LP 16 027
hannover november 1957	seemann, piano	lp: dg LPM 18 696/SLPM 138 696 cd: dg originals 463 6532

brahms/**violin sonata no 2**
vienna	wührer, piano	78: dg LVM 72 181-72 182
8-10		lp: dg LPM 18 144
january		lp: melodiya M10 46983 006
1952		cd: partita (japan) PC 9207-9208
		melodiya issue incorrectly dated 1942

hannover	seemann, piano	lp: dg LPM 18 633/SLPM 138 633/2535 751
6-12		cd: dg originals 463 6532
february		
1960		

violin sonata no 3
hannover	seemann, piano	lp: dg LPM 18 696/SLPM 138 696
november		cd: dg originals 463 6532
1957		

scherzo in c minor/fae sonata
hannover	seemann, piano	lp: dg LPM 18 633/SLPM 18 633/2535 751
6-12		cd: dg originals 463 6532
february		
1960		

hungarian dance no 5, arranged for violin and piano by joachim
vienna	schulhof, piano	78: columbia DB 1084
1934		cd: amadeo 431 3442/431 3432

salzburg	hirsch, piano	45: dg EPL 30 336
29-30		
july		
1957		

string quartet op 51 no 1
munich	strasser,	cd: amadeo 431 3462/431 3432
9 march	second violin	*bayerischer rundfunk*
1951	streng, viola	
	krotschak, cello	

brahms/**piano trio no 1**

salzburg 8 august 1953	fischer, piano mainardi, cello	lp: cetra DOC 35 *sender rot-weiss-rot*
munich 30 november 1953	fischer, piano mainardi, piano	lp: discocorp BWS 739 lp: music and arts CD 739 cd: amadeo 431 3472/431 3432 *bayerischer rundfunk*
rome 20 december 1953	fischer, piano mainardi, piano	unpublished radio broadcast *rai roma*
salzburg 4 august 1954	fischer, piano mainardi, cello	lp: cetra DOC 55 cd: arkadia CD 568/CDHP 568

piano trio no 2

munich 2 december 1951	fischer, piano mainardi, cello	lp: discocorp BWS 739 cd: music and arts CD 739 cd: amadeo 431 3472/431 3432 *bayerischer rundfunk*
salzburg 9 august 1952	fischer, piano mainardi, cello	unpublished radio brodcast *sender rot-weiss-rot*
rome 20 december 1953	fischer, piano mainardi, cello	unpublished radio broadcast *rai roma*
salzburg 4 august 1954	fischer, piano mainardi, cello	lp: cetra DOC 55 cd: arkadia CD 568/CDHP 568

piano trio no 3

salzburg 4 august 1954	fischer, piano mainardi, cello	lp: cetra DOC 55 cd: arkadia CD 568/CDHP 568

JOHANN BRANDL (1835-1913)
du alter stefansdom, arranged for violin and piano from the operetta der liebe augustin *also known as the old refrain*

munich werba, piano lp: emi SHZE 281
1-10
october
1969

MAX BRUCH (1838-1920)
violin concerto no 1

bamberg	bamberg	78: dg LVM 72 232-72 233
28-30	symphony	lp: dg LPM 18 036/LPE 17 028/LPEM 19 124
april	leitner	lp: dg heliodor 2548 024
1952		cd: dg original masters 477 5263
		cd: profil medien PH 4062

FREDERIC CHOPIN (1810-1849)
nocturne no 2, arranged for violin and piano by sarasate

salzburg hirsch, piano 45: dg EPL 30 337
29-30
july
1957

JEAN ANTOINE DESPLANES (1678-1704)
intrada, arranged for violin and piano by nachez

munich priegnitz, piano 45: dg NL 32 047/NL 36 084
4 april
1952

ANTONIN DVORAK (1841-1904)
violin sonatina in g

vienna klien, piano lp: dg 39 163/139 163
6-7
january
1965

EDWARD ELGAR (1857-1934)
la capricieuse, for violin and piano

salzburg hirsch, piano 45: dg EPL 30 336
29-30
july
1957

MANUEL DE FALLA (1876-1946)
danza espanola from la vida breve, arranged for violin and piano by kreisler

salzburg	hirsch, piano	45: dg EPL 30 337
29-30		
july		
1957		

ZDENEK FIBICH (1850-1900)
poeme, arranged for violin and piano by kubelik

vienna	schulhof, piano	78: columbia DB 1058
1934		78: columbia (germany) DW 4171
		78: columbia (norway) GN 108
		cd: amadeo 431 3442/431 3432
		cd: opus kura OPK 2020

CESAR FRANCK (1822-1890)
violin sonata in a

hannover	seemann, piano	lp: dg LPM 18 633/SLPM 138 633/2535 751
20-21		
february		
1960		

KARL AMADEUS HARTMANN (1905-1963)
concerto funebre for violin and strings

munich	bavarian radio	unpublished radio broadcast
11 december	orchestra	*bayerischer rundfunk*
1964	henze	

FRANZ JOSEF HAYDN (1732-1809)
string quartet op 76 no 5

munich	strasser,	cd: amadeo 431 3462/431 3432
29 october	second violin	*bayerischer rundfunk*
1950	streng, viola	
	krotschak, cello	

HANS WERNER HENZE (born 1926)
violin concerto

munich	bavarian radio	lp: dg 139 382
12-13	orchestra	cd: dg 449 8652/449 8602
may	henze	
1968		

ariosi for soprano, violin and orchestra

munich	bavarian radio	cd: amadeo 431 3482/431 3432
11 december	orchestra	*bayerischer rundfunk*
1964	henze	
	seefried	

PAUL HINDEMITH (1895-1963)
violin sonata no 3

vienna	seemann, piano	lp: dg LPM 18 400
6-9		lp: decca (usa) DL 9980
april		
1957		

WILLY KLASEN
berceuse for violin and piano

vienna	klasen, piano	78: hmv X 2718
1927		cd: amadeo 431 3442/431 3432

mazurka for violin and piano

vienna	klasen, piano	78: hmv X 2718
1927		cd: amadeo 431 3442/431 3432

FRITZ KREISLER (1875-1962)
caprice viennois for violin and piano

salzburg	hirsch, piano	45: dg EPL 30 335
29-30		
july		
1957		

munich	werba, piano	lp: emi SHZE 281
1-10		
october		
1969		

liebesfreud for violin and piano

salzburg	hirsch, piano	45: dg EPL 30 335
29-30		
july		
1957		

kreisler/**liebesleid for violin and piano**

salzburg 29-30 july 1957	hirsch, piano	45: dg EPL 30 335
munich 1-10 october 1969	werba, piano	lp: emi SHZE 281

schön rosmarin for violin and piano

munich 1-10 october 1969	werba, piano	lp: emi SHZE 281

ROLF LIEBERMANN (born 1910)
capriccio for soprano, violin and orchestra

vienna 14 september 1970	austrian radio orchestra horvath seefried	cd: amadeo 431 3482/431 3432 *österreichischer rundfunk*

FRANK MARTIN (1890-1974)
violin concerto

geneva 1955	suisse romande orchestra ansermet	lp: decca LX 3146 lp: london (usa) LD 9213 cd: decca 448 2642 cd: dg original masters 477 5263
cologne 10 june 1966	wdr orchestra dohnanyi	unpublished radio broadcast *westdeutscher rundfunk*
date uncertain	luxemburg radio orchestra martin	lp: candide CE 31055 cd: jecklin JD 6322

martin/**mariae triptychon for soprano, violin and orchestra**

rotterdam 14 november 1969	netherlands radio philharmonic fournet seefried	unpublished radio broadcast *nederlands radio*
london 8 july 1970	new philharmonia giulini seefried	unpublished radio broadcast *bbc london*
geneva 7 september 1970	suisse romande orchestra martin seefried	cd: jecklin JD 6452
vienna 14 september 1970	austrian radio orchestra horvath seefried	cd: amadeo 431 3482/431 3432 *österreichischer rundfunk*
hamburg 19 october 1970	ndr orchestra schmidt-isserstedt seefried	unpublished radio broadcast *norddeutscher rundfunk*
amsterdam 25 february 1971	concertgebouw orchestra jochum seefried	unpublished radio broadcast *nederlands radio*

BOHUSLAV MARTINU (1890-1959)
étude rhythmique no 4

salzburg 29-30 july 1957	hirsch, piano	45: dg EPL 30 337

FELIX MENDELSSOHN-BARTHOLDY (1809-1847)
violin concerto

berlin 19-23 september 1956	rso berlin fricsay	lp: dg LPE 17 085/LPEM 19 124 lp: dg heliodor 2548 024 cd: amadeo 431 3452/431 3432 cd: dg original masters 477 5028/477 5263

WOLFGANG AMADEUS MOZART (1756-1791)
violin concerto no 1 k207

berlin	berlin	lp: dg 139 464/139 350-139 352/2740 116
6-13	philharmonic	cd: dg 445 0212
february	*schneiderhan*	
1967	*conducts from the violin*	

violin concerto no 2 k211

berlin	berlin	lp: dg 139 445/139 350-139 352/2740 116
22 march	philharmonic	cd: dg 445 0212
1965	*schneiderhan*	
	conducts from the violin	

violin concerto no 3 k216

berlin	berlin	lp: dg 139 445/139 350-139 352/2740 116
6-13	philharmonic	cd: dg 429 1592
february	*schneiderhan*	cd: dg belart
1967	*conducts from the violin*	

mozart/**violin concerto no 4 k218**

berlin 13-14 march 1956	berlin philharmonic rosbaud	lp: dg LPM 18 314 lp: decca (usa) DL 9857 cd: dg original masters 457 7202
berlin 5 december 1960	berlin philharmonic schmidt-isserstedt	lp: dg LPE 17 255/LPM 18 678/ SLPM 138 678/2535 124
berlin 6-13 february 1967	berlin philharmonic *schneiderhan conducts from the violin*	lp: dg 139 350-139 352/2740 116 cd: dg 429 1592
cologne 17 february 1967	wdr orchestra dohnanyi	unpublished radio broadcast *westdeutscher rundfunk*
munich 12-13 march 1970	bavarian radio orchestra kubelik	cd: refrain (japan) *bayerischer rundfunk*

mozart/**violin concerto no 5 k219**

vienna 1944	vienna philharmonic knappertsbusch	unpublished radio broadcast *reichsrundfunk*
berlin 7 august 1944	städtische oper orchestra schmidt-isserstedt	unpublished radio broadcast *reichsrundfunk*
vienna 16 september 1952	vienna symphony leitner	lp: dg LP 16 060/LPM 18 314 lp: decca (usa) DL 9857 cd: dg original masters 477 5263 cd: profil medien PH 4062
berlin 2 november 1953	rias-orchester desarzens	cd: foyer CDS 16006
hamburg-harburg 24-25 may 1960	ndr orchestra schmidt-isserstedt	lp: dg LPM 18 678/SLPM 138 678/2535 124
frankfurt 14 october 1961	hessischer rundfunk orchestra schuricht	lp: king records (japan)
berlin 6-13 february 1967	berlin philharmonic *schneiderhan conducts from the violin*	lp: dg 139 350-139 352/2740 116 cd: dg 429 1592/447 4032
salzburg 4 august 1973	vienna philharmonic *schneiderhan conducts from the violin*	cd: amadeo 431 3492/431 3432 *österreichischer rundfunk*

mozart/**sinfonia concertante for violin and viola k364**
salzburg	vienna	cd: orfeo C301 921B
6 august	philharmonic	
1969	böhm	
	streng, viola	

adagio for violin and orchestra k261
berlin	berlin	lp: dg 139 464/139 350-139 352/2740 116
6-13	philharmonic	cd: dg 445 0212
february	*schneiderhan*	
1967	*conducts from the*	
	violin	

salzburg	vienna	cd: amadeo 431 3492/431 3432
4 august	philharmonic	*österreichischer rundfunk*
1973	*schneiderhan*	
	conducts from the	
	violin	

rondo for violin and orchestra k269
berlin	berlin	lp: dg 139 464/139 350-139 352/2740 116
6-13	philharmonic	cd: dg 445 0212
february	*schneiderhan*	
1967	*conducts from the*	
	violin	

salzburg	vienna	cd: amadeo 431 3492/431 3432
4 august	philharmonic	*österreichischer rundfunk*
1973	*schneiderhan*	
	conducts from the	
	violin	

rondo for violin and orchestra k373
berlin	berlin	lp: dg 139 464/139 350-139 352/2740 116
6-13	philharmonic	
february	*schneiderhan*	
1967	*conducts from the*	
	violin	

salzburg	vienna	cd: amadeo 431 3492/431 3432
4 august	philharmonic	*österreichischer rundfunk*
1973	*schneiderhan*	
	conducts from the	
	violin	

mozart/**non temer amato bene, aria for soprano with violin obbligato**
vienna	vienna symphony	78: dg LVM 72 351
15 september	leitner	45: dg EPL 30 045
1952	seefried	lp: dg NK 558-559
		lp: decca (usa) DL 9768/DL 9833
		cd: amadeo 431 3482/431 3432

munich	bavarian radio	unpublished radio broadcast
27 january	orchestra	*bayerischer rundfunk*
1956	jochum	
	seefried	

l'amero saro costante, aria for soprano with violin obbligato
vienna	vienna symphony	78: dg LVM 72 351
15 september	leitner	45: dg EPL 30 045
1952	seefried	lp: dg 410 8471
		lp: decca (usa) DL 9768/DL 9833
		cd: amadeo 431 3482/431 3432

würzburg	bavarian radio	unpublished radio broadcast
26 january	orchestra	*bayerischer rundfunk*
1956	jochum	
	seefried	

würzburg	bavarian radio	unpublished radio broadcasr
15 june	orchestra	*bayerischer rundfunk*
1956	jochum	
	seefried	

piano trio k548
salzburg	fischer, piano	lp: discocorp BWS 735
9 august	mainardi, cello	*sender rot-weiss-rot*
1952		

mozart/**string quartet k428**
munich   strasser,   cd: amadeo 431 3462/431 3432
29 october   second violin   *bayerischer rundfunk*
1951   streng, viola
                  krotschak, cello

string quartet k458 "hunt"
1949-1950   strasser,   cd: orfeo C402 951B
                  second violin
                  streng, viola
                  krotschak, cello

violin sonata no 17 k296
hannover   seemann, piano   lp: dg LPM 18 307
17 december
1954

violin sonata no 18 k301
vienna   seemann, piano   lp: dg LPM 18 323
6 october   lp: decca (usa) DL 9886
1955

violin sonata no 21 k304
vienna   seemann, piano   lp: dg LP 16 092/LPM 18 323
19 september   lp: decca (usa) DL 9886
1953

violin sonata no 22 k305
vienna   seemann, piano   lp: dg LPM 18 316
6 october
1955

violin sonata no 24 k376
hannover   seemann, piano   lp: dg LPM 18 316
18 december
1954

violin sonata no 25 k377
vienna   seemann, piano   lp: dg LPM 18 250
7-9   lp: decca (usa) DL 9862
october
1955

violin sonata no 26 k378
hannover   seemann, piano   lp: dg LPM 18 260
19 december
1954

mozart/**violin sonata no 27 k379**
vienna   seemann, piano   lp: dg LPM 18 260
19-21
september
1953

violin sonata no 28 k380
vienna   seemann, piano   lp: dg LP 16 092/LPM 18 323
19-21   lp: decca (usa) DL 9886
september
1953

violin sonata no 32 k454
vienna   seemann, piano   lp: dg LPM 18 250
22-25   lp: decca (usa) DL 9862
september
1953

schwetzingen   seemann, piano   cd: orfeo C473 971B
15 june
1964

violin sonata no 33 k481
hannover   seemann, piano   lp: dg LPM 18 307
17-18
december
1955

violin sonata no 34 k526
vienna   seemann, piano   lp: dg LPM 18 250
22-25
september
1953

mozart/**serenade no 13 "eine kleine nachtmusik"**
salzburg	vienna	cd: amadeo 431 3492/431 3432
4 august	philharmonic	*bayerischer tundfunk*
1973	*schneiderhan*	
	conducts	

string divertimento in f k138
salzburg	vienna	cd: amadeo 431 3492/431 3432
4 august	philharmonic	*bayerischer rundfunk*
1973	*schneiderhan*	
	conducts	

MODEST MUSSORGSKY (1839-1881)
hebrew song, arranged for violin and piano by hartmann
vienna	nordberg, piano	78: columbia LB 88
25 february		78: columbia (austria) LV 12
1949		

salzburg	hirsch, piano	45: dg EPL 30 337
29-30		
july		
1957		

gopak from sorotchinsky fair, arranged for violin and piano
salzburg	hirsch, piano	45: dg EPL 30 337
29-30		
july		
1957		

D.P. NASH
minuet in d for violin and piano
vienna	schulhof, piano	78: columbia DB 1084
1934		cd: amadeo 431 3442/431 3432

munich	priegnitz, piano	45: dg NL 32 047/NL 36 084
4 april		
1952		

SERGE PROKOFIEV (1891-1953)
violin sonata no 2
berlin	seemann, piano	lp: dg LPM 18 794/SLPM 138 794
10 february		cd: dg 445 4792
1961		

MAURICE RAVEL (1875-1937)
string quartet in f
1949-1950	strasser, second violin	cd: orfeo C402 951B
	streng, viola	
	krotschak, cello	

MAX REGER (1873-1916)
mariae wiegenlied for soprano, piano and violin obbligato
vienna	werba, piano	78: dg LV 62 893
september	seefried	45: dg NL 32 142
1953		lp: decca (usa) DL 7545

mariae wiegenlied, version with orchestra
munich	bayerisches	lp: emi SHZE 281
1-10	staatsorchester	
october	heger	
1969	seefried	

mariae wiegenlied, version for violin and piano
vienna	nordberg, piano	78: columbia LB 88
25 february		78: columbia (austria) LV 12
1949		

salzburg	hirsch, piano	45: dg EPL 30 336
29-30		
july		
1957		

FRANZ RIES (1846-1932)
perpetuum mobile from suite in g for violin and piano
vienna   schulhof, piano   78: columbia DX 477
1934   78: columbia (usa) 5124M
                                    cd: amadeo 431 3442/431 3432

salzburg   hirsch, piano   45: dg EPL 30 336
29-30
july
1957

CAMILLE SAINT-SAENS (1835-1921)
le cygne/le carnaval des animaux
vienna   schulhof, piano   78: columbia DB 1058
1934   78: columbia (germany) DW 4171
                                    78: columbia (norway) GN 108
                                    cd: amadeo 431 3442/431 3432
                                    cd: opus kura OPK 2020

munich   priegnitz, piano   45: dg NL 32 047/NL 36 084
4 april
1952

salzburg   hirsch, piano   45: dg EPL 30 335
29-30
july
1957

FRANZ ANTON SCHUBERT (1808-1878)
l'abeille/12 bagatelles for violin and piano
salzburg   hirsch, piano   45: dg EPL 30 336
29-30
july
1957

FRANZ SCHUBERT (1797-1828)
violin sonatina no 1 d384

vienna   seemann, piano   lp: dg LP 16 085/LPM 18 502
25-27
september
1953

vienna   klien, piano   lp: dg 39 101/139 101/2734 004
1965

violin sonatina no 2 d385

vienna   seemann, piano   lp: dg LPM 18 241
25-27
september
1953

vienna   klien, piano   lp: dg 39 101/139 101/2734 004/2535 225
1965

violin sonatina no 3 d408

vienna   seemann, piano   lp: dg LP 16 085/LPM 18 502
25-27
september
1953

vienna   klien, piano   lp: dg 39 101/139 101/2734 004
1965

fantasy in c for violin and piano d934

vienna   klien, piano   lp: dg 39 164/139 164/2734 004
9-10
december
1965

rondo brillant for violin and piano d895

vienna   klien, piano   lp: dg 39 164/139 164/2734 004
15 march
1966

schubert/**duo in a for violin and piano d574**
hannover 16 december 1954	seemann, piano	lp: dg LPM 18 241
schwetzingen 15 june 1964	seemann, piano	cd: orfeo C473 971B
vienna 9-10 december 1965	klien, piano	lp: dg 39 164/139 164/2734 004

piano trio no 2 d929
lucerne august 1954	fischer, piano mainardi, cello	unpublished private recording of rehearsal *classical recordings archive of america*

octet d803
vienna 12-15 december 1947	strasser, second violin moravec, viola krotschak, cello rühm, double-bass wlach, clarinet freiberg, horn öhlberger, bassoon	78: columbia (germany) LWX 364-369 *recording completed on 29 january 1949*

ROBERT SCHUMANN (1810-1856)
violin sonata no 1
vienna 11 december 1947	wührer, piano	78: columbia LX 1193 *second movement only*
hannover 18 december 1955	seemann, piano	45: dg EPL 30 206 lp: dg LPM 18 502 cd: dg 445 4792

piano trio no 1
salzburg 8 august 1954	fischer, piano mainardi, cello	lp: discocorp BWS 735 lp: cetra DOC 35 cd: arkadia CD 568/CDHP 568 *sender rot-weiss-rot*

RICHARD STRAUSS (1864-1949)
violin sonata in e flat

vienna 11 december 1965	klien, piano	lp: dg 39 163/139 163

morgen, orchestral song with violin obbligato

munich 1-10 october 1969	bayerisches staatsorchester heger seefried	lp: emi SHZE 281

IGOR STRAVINSKY (1882-1971)
violin concerto

berlin 3-5 december 1962	berlin philharmonic ancerl	lp: dg LPM 18 794/SLPM 138 794/135 155 cd: dg originals 463 6662

duo concertant for violin and piano

vienna 6-9 april 1957	seemann, piano	lp: dg LPM 18 400 lp: decca (usa) DL 9980

danse russe from petrushka, arranged for violin and piano by dushkin and stravinsky

salzburg 29-30 july 1957	hirsch, piano	45: dg EPL 30 334

russian maiden's song from mavra, arranged for violin and piano by dushkin and stravinsky

salzburg 29-30 july 1957	hirsch, piano	45: dg EPL 30 334

GIUSEPPE TARTINI (1692-1770)
violin concerto in d

lucerne 30-31 january 1957	lucerne festival strings baumgartner	45: dg archiv EPA 37 200 lp: dg archiv APM 14 115 lp: decca (usa) ARC 3117 cd: dg original masters 477 5263

PIOTR TCHAIKOVSKY (1840-1893)
violin concerto

prague	czech	78: columbia (germany) LWX 349-352
1940	philharmonic	cd: amadeo 431 3442/431 3432
	talich	cd: urania URN 22149

ANTONIO VIVALDI (1678-1741)
le 4 stagioni

vienna	lucerne festival	lp: dg archiv AP 13 076/SAP 195 008
2-6	strings	lp: dg 135 024/2535 105
october	baumgartner	lp: decca (usa) ARC 3141/ARC 73141
1958		cd: dg archiv 431 4792
		cd: dg original masters 477 5263

spring concerto only
lp: dg 2721 180

concerto no 3/l'estro armonico

salzburg	lucerne festival	45: dg archiv EPA 37 199/SEPA 181 199
4 august	strings	lp: dg archiv APM 14 097
1958	starck, cello	lp: dg 135 024
	baumgartner,	lp: decca (usa) ARC 3116
	second violin	cd: dg original masters 477 5263
	and conductor	

HUGO WOLF (1860-1903)
italian serenade

vienna	strasser,	78: columbia LX 1168
14 december	second violin	78: columbia (austria) LVX 45
1947	moravec, viola	
	krotschak, cello	

CONCERTGEBOUW – AMSTERDAM

WOENSDAG 22 OCTOBER / DONDERDAG 23 OCTOBER 1952 - 8.15 UUR

ABONNEMENTSCONCERT - SERIE B No. 2

HET CONCERTGEBOUWORKEST

Dirigent **Eduard van Beinum**
Solist **Arthur Grumiaux,** viool

PROGRAMMA

HENRY PURCELL - BLISS
1657-1695

Acttunes and Dances

Ouverture (Gordian Knot)
Air (Distressed Innocence)
Sarabande (Amphitryon)
Menuet (Distressed Innocence)
Hornpipe (the Married Beau)

BÉLA BARTÓK
1881-1945

Concert
VOOR VIOOL EN ORKEST

Allegro non troppo
Andante tranquillo
Allegro molto

PAUZE

L. VAN BEETHOVEN
1770-1827

Tweede symphonie D gr. t., op. 36

Adagio molto - Allegro con brio
Larghetto
Scherzo : Allegro
Allegro molto

concert playbills on this and subsequent pages by courtesy of roderick krüsemann

Seizoen 1966/67 **Concertgebouworkest**
Concertgebouw - Amsterdam
zondag 22 januari 1967 - 14.15 uur

serie Z nr. 4 Abonnementsconcert

---

dirigent Pierre Boulez
solist Arthur Grumiaux, viool

---

programma

Joseph Haydn * Symfonie nr. 13, in D gr. t. (1763)
1732-1809
    Allegro molto
    Adagio cantabile
    Menuet
    Finale: Allegro molto

Alban Berg Concert (1935)
1885-1935 voor viool en orkest
    Andante - Allegretto
    Allegro - Adagio

pauze

Robert Schumann Tweede symfonie in C gr. t., op. 61 (1845/46)
1810-1856
    Sostenuto assai - Allegro ma non troppo
    Scherzo: Allegro vivace
    Adagio espressivo
    Allegro molto vivace

CONCERTGEBOUW - AMSTERDAM

WOENSDAG 27 NOVEMBER / DONDERDAG 28 NOVEMBER 1957 - 8.15 UUR

ABONNEMENTSCONCERT - SERIE B Nr. 7

HET CONCERTGEBOUWORKEST

Dirigent **George Szell**
Solist **Arthur Grumiaux**, viool

PROGRAMMA

HECTOR BERLIOZ
1803-1869

Ouverture „Benvenuto Cellini" (1838)

FRANZ SCHUBERT
1797-1828

Symfonie b kl. t. (1822)
„Onvoltooide"
Allegro moderato
Andante con moto

W. A. MOZART
1756-1791

Concert, Bes gr. t., K.V. 207 (1775)
VOOR VIOOL EN ORKEST
Allegro moderato
Adagio
Presto

Cadenzen van Arthur Grumiaux

Pauze

ERNEST CHAUSSON
1855-1899

Poème, op. 25 (1896)
VOOR VIOOL EN ORKEST

MAURICE RAVEL
1875-1937

La Valse (1920)
POÈME CHORÉGRAPHIQUE

CONCERTGEBOUW - AMSTERDAM

ABONNEMENTSCONCERT - SERIE C Nr. 1

ZONDAG 26 OKTOBER 1958 / 2.30 UUR

HET CONCERTGEBOUWORKEST

Dirigent **Eduard van Beinum**
Solist **Wolfgang Schneiderhan**, viool

PROGRAMMA

G. F. HANDEL   **Concerto grosso, g kl. t., op. 6 nr. 6 (1739)**
1685-1759
VOOR STRIJKORKEST EN BASSO CONTINUO

Largo affettuoso
A tempo giusto
Musette: Larghetto
Allegro
Allegro

Concertino: **Jacob Krachmalnick** en **Jan Bresser**, viool;
Tibor de Machula, violoncel

W. A. MOZART   **Vierde concert, D gr. t., K.V. 218 (1775)**
1756-1791
VOOR VIOOL EN ORKEST

Allegro
Andante cantabile
Rondeau: Andante grazioso - Allegro ma non troppo

Cadenzen van Wolfgang Schneiderhan

Pauze

GEORGES BIZET   **Petite Suite (Jeux d'enfants), op. 22 (1871)**
1838-1875

Marche (Trompette et tambour)
Berceuse (La poupée)
Impromptu (La toupie)
Duo (Petit mari, petite femme)
Galop (Le Bal)

MAURICE RAVEL   **La Valse (1920)**
1875-1937
POÈME CHORÉGRAPHIQUE

CONCERTGEBOUW - AMSTERDAM

WOENSDAG 31 OKTOBER / DONDERDAG 1 NOVEMBER 1962 - 20.15 UUR

ABONNEMENTSCONCERT SERIE B - Nr. 4

HET CONCERTGEBOUWORKEST

Dirigent **Eugen Jochum**
Solist **Wolfgang Schneiderhan,** viool

PROGRAMMA

PAUL HINDEMITH
Geb. 1895

Concert voor orkest, op. 38 (1925)
Mit Kraft, mässig schnelle Viertel
Sehr schnelle Halbe
Marsch für Holzbläser: Nicht zu langsame Viertel
Basso ostinato: Schnelle Viertel

W. A. MOZART
1756-1791

Vijfde concert, A gr. t., K.V. 219 (1775)
VOOR VIOOL EN ORKEST

Allegro aperto
Adagio
Rondeau: Tempo di Menuetto - Allegro - Tempo di Menuetto

Cadenzen van Joseph Joachim

Pauze

JOHANNES BRAHMS
1833-1897

Tweede symfonie, D gr. t., op. 73 (1877)
Allegro non troppo
Adagio non troppo
Allegretto grazioso (quasi andantino) - Presto ma non assai - Tempo primo
Allegro con spirito

arthur grumiaux
1921-1986
the discography

ISAAC ALBENIZ (1860-1909)
tango in d, arranged for violin and piano by kreisler

amsterdam 12 december 1962	hajdu, piano	lp: philips A02294L cd: philips original masters 473 1042
12-16 february 1973	hajdu, piano	lp: philips 6599 372-373 cd: philips 420 8182/446 6502

JOHANN SEBASTIAN BACH (1685-1750)
violin concerto no 1 bwv1041

amsterdam june 1955	chamber orchestra guller	lp: philips NBR 6032/N00782R lp: philips classical favourites G05326R lp: philips fontana weltserie 695 023KL lp: epic (usa) LC 3342
london june 1964	english chamber orchestra leppard	lp: philips AL 3489/SAL 3489/A02376L/ 835 254AY/6530 004 lp: philips festivo SFM 23022/839 557VGY lp: philips (usa) PHM 500 075/PHS 900 075
vevey 6-9 november 1978	les solistes romands gerecz	lp: philips 9500 614 cd: philips 420 7002/420 8892

bach/violin concerto no 2 bwv1042

amsterdam june 1955	chamber orchestra guller	lp: philips NBR 6032/N00782R lp: philips classical favourites G05326R lp: philips fontana weltserie 695 023KL lp: epic (usa) LC 3342

london
june
1964
	english chamber
	orchestra
	leppard
		lp: philips AL 3489/SAL 3489/A02376L/
		    835 254AY/SBAL 32/6530 004/
		    7CAX 403/SC71AX 403
		lp: philips festivo SFM 23022/839 557VGY
		lp: philips (usa) PHM 500 075/PHS 900 075

vevey 6-9 november 1978	les solistes romands gerecz	lp: philips 9500 614 cd: philips 420 7002

concerto for two violins bwv1043

london 27 march 1946	philharmonia susskind pougnet, second violin	78: columbia DX 1276-1277 78: columbia (italy) GQX 11320-11321 78: columbia (australia) DOX 854-855 78: columbia (france) GFX 124-125
wembley 1-5 september 1970	new philharmonia de waart toyoda, second violin	lp: philips 6500 119/6500 456
vevey 6-9 november 1978	les solistes romands gerecz krebbers, second violin	lp: philips 9500 614 cd: philips 420 7002

concerto for violin and oboe bwv1060

wembley 1-5 september 1970	new philharmonia de waart holliger, oboe	lp: philips 6500 119/6500 456 cd: philips 420 7002

bach/**solo violin sonata no 1 bwv1001**
berlin
24-27
november
1960

lp: philips AL 3472/SAL 3472/A02205L/
 835 198AY/6768 017
lp: philips (usa) PHM2-500/PHS2-900
cd: philips 416 8792/438 7362

solo violin partita no 1 bwv1002
berlin
july
1961

lp: philips AL 3472/SAL 3472/A-2205L/
 835 198AY/6768 017
lp: philips (usa) PHM2-500/PHS2-900
cd: philips 416 8792/438 7362

solo violin sonata no 2 bwv1003
berlin
march
1961

lp: philips AL 3473/SAL 3473/A02206L/
 835 199AY/6768 017
lp: philips (usa) PHM2-500/PHS2-900
cd: philips 416 8792/438 7362

solo violin partita no 2 bwv1004
berlin
march
1961

lp: philips AL 3473/SAL 3473/A02206L/
 835 199AY/6768 017
lp: philips (usa) PHM2-500/PHS2-900
cd: philips 416 8792/438 7362

chaconne from solo violin partita no 2
boston
1953

lp: boston B 202
lp: argo RG 109

paris
21 march
1967

dvd video: emi classic archive DVB 490 4459

sarabande from solo violin partita no 2
amsterdam
14 may
1962

dvd video: emi classic archive DVB 490 4459

solo violin sonata no 3 bwv1005
berlin
july
1961

lp: philips AL 3474/SAL 3474/A02207L/
 835 200AY/6768 017
lp: philips (usa) PHM2-500/PHS2-900
cd: philips 416 8792/438 7362

solo violin partita no 3 bwv1006
berlin
24-27
november
1960

lp: philips AL 3474/SAL 3474/A02207L/
 835 200AY/6768 017
lp: philips (usa) PHM2-500/PHS2-900
cd: philips 416 8792/438 7362

bach/sonata no 1 for violin and keyboard bwv1014

june 1963	sartori, harpsichord	lp: philips AL 3487/SAL 3487/A02349L/ 835 227AY lp: philips (usa) PHM2-597/PHS2-997
18-23 february 1978	jaccottet, harpsichord	lp: philips 9500 571/6769 017 cd: philips 426 4522/454 0112

sonata no 2 for violin and keyboard bwv1015

september 1963	sartori, harpsichord	lp: philips AL 3487/SAL 3487/A02349L/ 835 227AY lp: philips (usa) PHM2-597/PHS2-997
18-23 february 1978	jaccottet, harpsichord	lp: philips 9500 571/6769 017 cd: philips 426 4522/454 0112

sonata no 3 for violin and keyboard bwv1016

june 1963	sartori, harpsichord	lp: philips AL 3487/SAL 3487/A02349L/ 835 227AY lp: philips (usa) PHM2-597/PHS2-997
18-23 february 1978	jaccottet, harpsichord	lp: philips 9500 571/6769 017 cd: philips 426 4522/454 0112

sonata no 4 for violin and keyboard bwv1017

june 1963	sartori, harpsichord	lp: philips AL 3488/SAL 3488/A02350L/ 835 228AY lp: philips (usa) PHM2-597/PHS2-997
18-23 february 1978	jaccottet, harpsichord	lp: philips 9500 572/6769 017 cd: philips 426 4522/454 0112

sonata no 5 for violin and keyboard bwv1018

september 1963	sartori, harpsichord	lp: philips AL 3488/SAL 3488/A02350L/ 835 228AY lp: philips (usa) PHM2-597/PHS2-997
18-23 february 1978	jaccottet, harpsichord	lp: philips 9500 572/6769 017 cd: philips 426 4522/454 0112

bach/**sonata no 6 for violin and keyboard   bwv1019**
september	sartori,	lp:	philips AL 3488/SAL 3488/A02350L/
1963	harpsichord		835 228AY
		lp:	philips (usa) PHM2-597/PHS2-997

18-23	jaccottet,	lp:	philips 9500 572/6769 017
february	harpsichord	cd:	philips 426 4522/454 0112
1978			

sonata no 7 for violin and keyboard   bwv 1019a
9-14	jaccottet,	lp:	philips 9500 905
april	harpsichord		
1980	mermoud, cello		

sonata no 8 for violin and keyboard   bwv1020
9-14	jaccottet,	lp:	philips 9500 905
april	harpsichord		
1980	mermoud, cello		

sonata no 9 for violin and keyboard   bwv1021
9-14	jaccottet,	lp:	philips 9500 905
april	harpsichord		
1980	mermoud, cello		

sonata no 10 for violin and keyboard   bwv1022
9-14	jaccottet,	lp:	philips 9500 905
april	harpsichord		
1980	mermoud, cello		

sonata no 11 for violin and keyboard   bwv1023
9-14	jaccottet,	lp:	philips 9500 905
april	harpsichord		
1980	mermoud, cello		

BELA BARTOK (1881-1945)
rumanian folkdances, arranged for violin and piano by szekely
1953   ulanowsky, piano   lp: boston records B 203

LUDWIG VAN BEETHOVEN (1770-1827)
violin concerto

amsterdam	concertgebouw	lp: philips L00434L
4 june	orchestra	lp: philips fontana 6530 018
1957	van beinum	lp: philips fontana grandioso 894 048ZKY
		lp: eterna 820 126
		lp: epic (usa) LC 3420
paris	orchestre	dvd video: emi classic archive DVB 490 4459
4 february	national	
1965	dorati	
wembley	new	lp: philips AL 3616/SAL 3616/L02719L/
3-5	philharmonia	A02822L/802 719LY/802 822AY/
july	galliera	SBAL 32/7CAX 403/SC71AX 403
1966		lp: philips (usa) PHS 900 222
		cd: philips 426 0642
amsterdam	concertgebouw	lp: philips 6500 775
7-9	orchestra	cd: philips 420 3482/442 2872
january	davis	
1974		

violin romance no 1

amsterdam	concertgebouw	45: philips ABE 10268/SABE 2028/400 211AE
11-14	orchestra	lp: philips classical favourites G05406R
may	haitink	lp: philips fontana 6570 051
1960		lp: philips fontana grandioso 894 069ZKY
		lp: epic (usa) LC 3762/BC 1120
		cd: philips 442 5772
wembley	new	lp: philips universo 6580 047
12-14	philharmonia	cd: philips 420 3482/426 0642
october	de waart	
1970		

beethoven/**violin romance no 2**

amsterdam	concertgebouw	45: philips ABE 10268/SABE 2028/400 211AE
11-14	orchestra	lp: philips classical favourites G05406R
may	haitink	lp: philips fontana 6570 051
1960		lp: philips fontana grandioso 894 069ZKY
		lp: epic (usa) LC 3762/BC 1120
		cd: philips 442 5772
wembley	new	lp: philips universo 6580 047
12-14	philharmonia	cd: philips 420 3482/426 0642
october	de waart	
1970		

violin sonata op 12 no 1

july	kapell, piano	lp: discocorp RR 547
1955		cd: stradivarius STR 10020
amsterdam	haskil, piano	lp: philips ABL 3204/A00409L/A00790R/
2-5		836 962DSY/6733 001
january		lp: philips classical favourites GL 5858
1957		lp: philips universo 6580 090
		lp: epic (usa) LC 3400/SC 6030
		cd: philips 422 1402/442 6252/442 6852
amsterdam	arrau, piano	lp: philips 9500 055
24-31		
march		
1975		

beethoven/**violin sonata op 12 no 2**

amsterdam 16-18 september 1956	haskil, piano	lp: philips ABL 3199/A00400L/836 961DSY/ 6733 001 lp: philips classical favourites GL 5857 lp: philips universo 6580 080 lp: epic (usa) LC 3488/SC 6030 cd: philips 422 1402/442 6252/442 6852
besancon 18 september 1957	haskil, piano	lp: discocorp RR 555 cd: melodram MEL 18001
amsterdam 13-17 april 1976	arrau, piano	lp: philips 9500 263 cd: philips 442 6512

violin sonata op 12 no 3

amsterdam 16-18 september 1956	haskil, piano	lp: philips ABL 3199/A00400L/836 961DSY/ 6733 001 lp: philips classical favourites GL 5857 lp: philips universo 6580 090 lp: epic (usa) LC 3488/SC 6030 cd: philips 422 1402/442 6252/442 6852
besancon 18 september 1957	haskil, piano	cd: melodram MEL 18001 cd: music and arts CD 860

violin sonata op 23

amsterdam 2-5 january 1957	haskil, piano	lp: philips ABL 3204/A00409L/A00709R/ 836 962DSY/6733 001 lp: philips classical favourites GL 5858 lp: philips universo 6580 090 lp: epic (usa) LC 3400/SC 6030 cd: philips 422 1402/442 6252/442 6852
ascona 22 august 1960	haskil, piano	cd: ermitage ERM 112
amsterdam 13-17 april 1976	arrau, piano	lp: philips 9500 263 cd: philips 442 6512

beethoven/**violin sonata op 24 "spring"**

amsterdam 2-5 january 1957	haskil, piano	lp: philips ABL 3204/A00409L/836 962DSY/ 6733 001 lp: philips classical favourites GL 5858 lp: philips fontana weltserie 695 073KL lp: philips universo 6580 032 lp: epic (usa) LC 3400/SC 6030 cd: philips 422 1402/442 6252/442 6852
amsterdam 24-31 march 1976	arrau, piano	lp: philips 9600 055 cd: philips 442 6512

violin sonata op 30 no 1

amsterdam 26-28 september 1957	haskil, piano	lp: philips ABL 3226/A00430L/836 964DSY/ 6733 001 lp: philips classical favourites GL 5860 lp: epic (usa) LC 3458/SC 6030 cd: philips 422 1402/442 6252/442 6852

violin sonata op 30 no 2

amsterdam 28-30 december 1956	haskil, piano	lp: philips ABL 3207/A00412L/836 963DSY/ 6733 001 lp: philips classical favourites GL 5859 lp: epic (usa) LC 3381/SC 6030 cd: philips 422 1402/442 6252/442 6852
amsterdam 16-20 may 1976	arrau, piano	lp: philips 9500 220

beethoven/**violin sonata op 30 no 3**

amsterdam 16-18 september 1956	haskil, piano	lp: philips ABL 3199/A00400L/836 961DSY/ 6733 001 lp: philips classical favourites GL 5857 lp: philips universo 6580 032 lp: epic (usa) LC 3488/SC 6030 cd: philips 422 1402/442 6252/442 6852
amsterdam 16-20 may 1976	arrau, piano	lp: philips 9500 220 cd: philips 442 6512

violin sonata op 47 "kreutzer"

besancon 18 september 1957	haskil, piano	cd: melodram MEL 18001
amsterdam 26-28 september 1957	haskil, piano	lp: philips ABL 3226/A00430L/836 964DSY/ 6733 001 lp: philips classical favourites GL 5860/ GBR 6536/G05351R lp: philips fontana weltserie 695 073KL lp: philips universo 6580 032 lp: epic (usa) LC 3458/SC 6030 cd: philips 422 1402/442 6252/442 6852

violin sonata op 96

amsterdam 28-30 december 1956	haskil, piano	lp: philips ABL 3207/A00412L/836 963DSY/ 6733 001 lp: philips classical favourites GL 5859 lp: epic (usa) LC 3381/SC 6030 cd: philips 422 1402/442 6252/442 6852
besancon 18 september 1957	haskil, piano	lp: discocorp RR 555 cd: melodram MEL 18001 cd: music and arts CD 860
ascona 22 august 1960	haskil, piano	cd: ermitage ERM 112

beethoven/**string trio no 1**
september	janzer, viola	lp: philips 6500 168/6768 034/SC71AX 309
1968	czako, cello	lp: philips (usa) PHS 900 226
		cd: philips 456 3172

string trio no 2
3-11	janzer, viola	lp: philips 6500 168/6768 034/SC71AX 309
january	czako, cello	lp: philips (usa) PHS 900 226
1968		cd: philips 456 3172

string trio no 3
september	janzer, viola	lp: philips SC71AX 309/6768 034
1968	czako, cello	cd: philips 456 3172

string trio no 4
3-11	janzer, viola	lp: philips SC71AX 309/6768 034
january	czako, cello	cd: philips 456 3172
1968		

string serenade op 8
3-11	janzer, viola	lp: philips 6500 167/6768 034/SC71AX 309
january	czako, cello	lp: philips (usa) PHS 900 227
1968		

flute serenade op 25
8-9	larrieu, flute	lp: philips 6500 167/6768 034/SC71AX 309
may	janzer, viola	lp: philips (usa) PHS 900 227
1968		cd: philips 454 2472

minuet in g for violin and piano
12-16	hajdu, piano	cd: philips 446 6502
february		*unpublished philips lp recording*
1973		

ALBAN BERG (1885-1935)
violin concerto

amsterdam	concertgebouw	lp: philips SAL 3650/802 785LY
23-25	orchestra	lp: philips (france) 6555 078
january	markevitch	lp: philips (usa) PHS 900 194
1967		cd: philips 422 1362

HECTOR BERLIOZ (1803-1869)
reverie et caprice pour violon et orchestre

wembley	new	lp: philips 6768 304
12-14	philharmonia	lp: philips universo 6580 047
october	de waart	cd: philips 456 1432
1970		

ERNEST BLOCH (1880-1959)
baal shem from nigun

december	hajdu, piano	cd: philips 446 6502
1962		*unpublished philips lp recording*

paris	chometon, piano	dvd video: emi classic archive DVB 490 4459
21 march		
1967		

JOHANNES BRAHMS (1833-1897)
violin concerto

amsterdam	concertgebouw	lp: philips AL 3526/SABL 141/SAL 3526/
3-4	orchestra	L09007L/A02356L/A02823L/835 008AY/
july	van beinum	835 234LY/SBAL 32/SC71AX 403
1958		lp: philips diskothek der meister 610 105VR/
		836 255VZ
		lp: philips classical favourites G05461R
		lp: epic (usa) LC 3552

walthamstow	new	lp: philips 6500 299
7-10	philharmonia	lp: philips sequenza 6527 197
september	davis	cd: philips 420 7032/442 2872
1971		

double concerto

milan	rai milano	cd: stradivarius STR 10013
12 april	orchestra	
1964	monteux	
	janigro, cello	

brahms/**violin sonata no 1**

15-19 february 1976	sebok, piano	lp: philips 9500 161 lp: philips fontana 6570 880 cd: philips 446 5702

violin sonata no 2

amsterdam october 1959	grumiaux, piano	lp: philips A02078L/802 839LY *violin and piano parts were recorded separately*
9-12 september 1975	sebok, piano	lp: philips 9500 108 lp: philips fontana 6570 880 cd: philips 446 5702

violin sonata no 3

9-12 september 1975	sebok, piano	lp: philips 9500 108 lp: philips fontana 6570 880 cd: philips 446 5702

horn trio in e flat

1953	stagliano, horn tucker, piano	lp: boston records B 209
15-19 february 1976	orval, horn sebok, piano	lp: philips 9500 161 cd: philips 438 3652/454 0732

MAX BRUCH (1838-1920)
violin concerto no 1

vienna 29 october- 1 november 1956	vienna symphony leskovich	lp: philips A00422L lp: epic (usa) LC 3365

amsterdam
17-18
july
1962
	concertgebouw
	orchestra
	haitink
		lp: philips AL 3526/SAL 3526/A02356L/
		    835 234LY/838 127DXY
		lp: philips diskothek der meister 610 124VR/
		    836 234VZ
		lp: philips fontana grandioso 894 100ZKY
		lp: philips universo 6580 022

wembley 20-23 september 1973	new philharmonia wallberg	lp: philips 6500 780 lp: philips sequenza 6527 122 cd: philips 420 7032

scottish fantasy for violin and orchestra

wembley 20-23 september 1973	new philharmonia wallberg	lp: philips 6500 780 lp: philips sequenza 6527 122

ERNEST CHAUSSON (1855-1899)
poeme pour violon et orchestre

paris 21-22 june 1954	orchestre lamoureux fournet	lp: philips ABL 3126/A00228L lp: philips classical favourites G03032L lp: philips fontana weltserie 695 092KL lp: epic (usa) LC 3082 cd: philips original masters 473 1042
paris march 1966	orchestre lamoureux rosenthal	lp: philips SAL 3587/802 708LY/ SBAL 32/6768 304 lp: philips (usa) PHS 900 195 cd: philips 416 8862

ARCANGELO CORELLI (1653-1713)
12 sonatas for violin and keyboard op 5

15-25 january 1975	castagnone, harpsichord	lp: philips 6700 096/6768 178

sonata no 12 "la follia"/12 sonatas op 5

amsterdam 16-19 july 1956	castagnone, harpsichord	lp: philips A00380L lp: epic (usa) LC 3414 cd: philips 438 5162

CLAUDE DEBUSSY (1862-1918)
violin sonata

1953	ulanowsky, piano	lp: boston records B 203
amsterdam 12-15 december 1955	castagnone, piano	lp: philips A00348L lp: epic (usa) LC 3667 cd: philips 438 5162
amsterdam july 1962	hajdu, piano	lp: philips AL 3644/SAL 3644/A02264L/ 835 174AY/802 770LY cd: philips 442 6552 cd: philips original masters 473 1042

ANTONIN DVORAK (1841-1904)
larghetto from violin sonatina in g

amsterdam 12-16 february 1973	hajdu, piano	lp: philips 6599 372-373 cd: philips 446 6502

humoresque in g flat

amsterdam 12-16 february 1973	hajdu, piano	lp: philips 6599 372-373 cd: philips 420 8182/446 6502

songs my mother taught me, arranged for violin and piano by kreisler

amsterdam 12-16 february 1973	hajdu, piano	lp: philips 6599 372-373 cd: philips 446 6502

EDWARD ELGAR (1857-1934)
la capricieuse, for violin and piano

amsterdam	hajdu, piano	lp: philips 6599 372-373
12-16		cd: philips 446 6502
february		
1973		

MANUEL DE FALLA (1876-1946)
jota from 7 popular spanish songs, arranged for violin and piano by kochanski

london	degraux, piano	78: columbia DX 2557/DC 422
6-7		
february		
1947		

danza espanola from la vida breve, arranged for violin and piano by kreisler

london	degraux, piano	78: columbia DX 1634/DCX 74
6 june		78: columbia (italy) GQX 16631
1946		

GABRIEL FAURE (1845-1924)
violin sonata no 1

amsterdam	hajdu, piano	lp: philips A02264L/835 174AY
july		cd: philips original masters 473 1042
1962		

14-18	crossley, piano	lp: philips 9500 534/412 3971
november		cd: philips 420 2632
1977		

violin sonata no 2

14-18	crossley, piano	lp: philips 9500 534/412 3971
november		cd: philips 420 3632
1977		

apres un reve, arranged for violin and piano

amsterdam	hajdu, piano	lp: philips 6599 372-373
12-16		cd: philips 446 6502
february		
1973		

les berceaux, for violin and piano

amsterdam	hajdu, piano	lp: philips A02294L
12 december		cd: philips 446 6502
1962		cd: philips original masters 473 1042

JOSEPH HECTOR FIOCCO (1703-1741)
allegro from harpsichord suite no 1, arranged for violin and piano by o'neill

london 6 august 1946	greenslade, piano	78: columbia DB 2488
1953	tucker, piano	lp: boston records B 202 lp: argo RG 109
amsterdam december 1962	hajdu, piano	lp: philips A02294L cd: philips 446 6502 cd: philips original masters 473 1042

CESAR FRANCK (1822-1890)
violin sonata

amsterdam december 1961	hajdu, piano	lp: philips AL 3738/SAL 3738/A02236L/ 835 342AY
16-19 may 1978	crossley, piano	lp: philips 9500 568 cd: philips 420 2632

CHRISTOPH WILLIBALD GLUCK (1714-1787)
dance of the blessed spirits from orfeo ed euridice, arranged for violin and piano by kreisler

amsterdam 12-16 february 1973	hajdu, piano	lp: philips 6599 372-373 cd: philips 446 5602

CHARLES GOUNOD (1818-1893)
ave maria, arranged for violin and piano

amsterdam 12-16 february 1973	hajdu, piano	lp: philips 6599 372-373 cd: philips 446 5602

ENRIQUE GRANADOS (1867-1916)
andaluza from danzas espanolas, arranged for violin and piano by kreisler

london 6 june 1946	degraux, piano	78: columbia DX 1634/DCX 74 78: columbia (italy) GQX 16631
amsterdam 12 december 1962	hajdu, piano	lp: philips A02294L cd: philips original masters 473 1042
amsterdam 12-16 february 1973	hajdu, piano	lp: philips 6599 372-373 cd: philips 420 8182/446 6502

EDVARD GRIEG (1843-1907)
violin sonata no 3

amsterdam december 1961	hajdu, piano	lp: philips AL 3738/SAL 3738/A02236L/ 835 342LY
16-19 may 1978	sebok, piano	lp: philips 9500 568

GEORGE FRIDERIC HANDEL (1685-1759)
sonatas for violin and keyboard op 1, nos 3, 10, 12, 13, 14 and 15

2-5 january 1966	veyron-lacroix, harpsichord	lp: philips SAL 3687/835 389AY/9502 023

FRANZ JOSEF HAYDN (1732-1809)
violin concerto no 1

london june 1964	english chamber orchestra leppard	lp: philips AL 3489/SAL 3489/A02376L/ 835 254AY/802 781DXY lp: philips festivo SFM 23022/839 557VGY lp: philips fontana 6530 004 lp: philips (usa) PHM 500 075/PHS 900 075

violin concerto no 2

wembley 5-11 april 1967	new philharmonia leppard	lp: philips SAL 3660/802 848LY

haydn/**string trio no 1**
february   janzer, viola   lp: philips SAL 3782/802 905LY
1969   czako, cello

string trio no 2
february   janzer, viola   lp: philips SAL 3782/802 905LY
1969   czako, cello

string trio no 3
february   janzer, viola   lp: philips SAL 3782/802 905LY
1969   czako, cello

MICHAEL HAYDN (1737-1806)
violin concerto in a
amsterdam   concertgebouw   lp: philips SAL 3804/839 757LY/6515 002
october   orchestra
1969   de waart

FRANZ HOFFMEISTER (1754-1812)
duet no 3 for violin and viola
21-25   pelliccia, viola   lp: philips 839 747LY
june
1968

JOSEPH JONGEN (1873-1953)
serenata for violin and piano
london   degraux, piano   78: columbia DC 421
6-7
february
1947

ZOLTAN KODALY (1882-1967)
adagio for violin and piano
amsterdam   hajdu, piano   cd: philips 446 6502
december   *unpublished philips lp recording*
1962

FRITZ KREISLER (1875-1962)
andante in the style of padre martin, for violin and piano
amsterdam 12-16 february 1973	hajdu, piano	lp: philips 6599 372-373 cd: philips 446 6502

caprice viennois for violin and piano
date uncertain	castagnone, piano	45: philips 402 138NE lp: philips classical favourites G05372R lp: epic (usa) LC 3592 cd: philips 438 5162

liebesfreud for violin and piano
date uncertain	castagnone, piano	45: philips 402 138NE lp: philips classical favourites G05372R lp: epic (usa) LC 3592 cd: philips 438 5162
amsterdam 12-16 february 1973	hajdu, piano	lp: philips 6599 372-373 cd: philips 420 8182/446 6502

liebesleid for violin and piano
date uncertain	castagnone, piano	45: philips 402 138NE lp: philips classical favourites G05372R lp: epic (usa) LC 3592 cd: philips 438 5162
amsterdam 12-16 february 1973	hajdu, piano	lp: philips 6599 372-373 cd: philips 420 8182/446 6502

rondino on a theme of beethoven, for violin and piano
amsterdam 12 december 1962	hajdu, piano	lp: philips A02294L
amsterdam 12-16 february 1973	hajdu, piano	lp: philips 6599 372-373 cd: philips 446 6502

kreisler/**schön rosmarin for violin and piano**
amsterdam	hajdu, piano	lp: philips 6599 372-373
12-16		cd: philips 420 8182/438 5162/446 6502
february		
1973		

tambourin chinois for violin and piano
date	castagnone, piano	45: philips 402 138NE
uncertain		lp: philips classical favourites G05372R
		lp: epic (usa) LC 3592
		cd: philips 438 5162

EDOUARD LALO (1823-1892)
symphonie espagnole pour violon et orchestre
paris	orchestre	lp: philips ABL 3126/A00228L
21-22	lamoureux	lp: philips fontana weltserie 695 091KL
june	fournet	lp: epic (usa) LC 3082
1954		cd: philips original masters 473 1042

paris	orchestre	lp: philips AL 3587/SAL 3587/A02309L/
1-5	lamoureux	835 184LY/802 824AY/6768 304/
april	rosenthal	SBAL 32/SC71AX 403
1963		lp: philips fontana 6570 192
		cd: philips 416 8862

JEAN-MARIE LECLAIR (1697-1764)
violin sonata op 9 no 3
amsterdam	hajdu, piano	lp: philips 6500 879
10-15		
june		
1974		

tambourin for violin and keyboard
amsterdam	hajdu, piano	lp: philips 6599 372-373
12-16		cd: philips 446 6502
february		
1973		

GUILLAUME LEKEU (1870-1894)
violin sonata in g

amsterdam 12-15 december 1955	castagnone, piano	lp: philips A00348L lp: epic (usa) LC 3667 cd: philips 438 5162
8-11 december 1973	varsi, piano	lp: philips 6500 814 lp: musique en wallonie MW 14

JULES MASSENET (1842-1912)
méditation de thais, arranged for violin and piano by marsick

amsterdam 12-16 february 1973	hajdu, piano	lp: philips 6599 372-373 cd: philips 446 6502

FELIX MENDELSSOHN-BARTHOLDY (1809-1847)
violin concerto

london 13-14 december 1946	philharmonia galliera	78: columbia (switzerland) DZX 25-28 78: columbia (italy) GQX 11126-11129
frankfurt february 1953	hessischer rundfunk orchestra giulini	cd: archipel ARPCD 0145
vienna 25-27 november 1953	vienna symphony moralt	lp: philips A00750R/S06112R/S04033L lp: philips classical favourites GBL 5582/ G03001L lp: philips fontana weltserie 695 015KL lp: epic (usa) LC 3173 cd: philips original masters 473 1042 *philips original masters incorrectly dated 1954*

amsterdam
11-14
may
1960
	concertgebouw
	orchestra
	haitink
		lp: philips ABL 3337/AL 3671/SABL 176/
		    SAL 3671/A02051L/A02821L/835 055AY/
		    802 821AY/SBAL 32/SC71AX 403
		lp: philips diskothek der meister 610 101VR/
		    836 215VZ
		lp: philips universo 6580 022
		lp: epic (usa) LC 3762/BC 1120
		cd: philips 442 2872/456 0742

nice 22 january 1961	orchestre national rosenthal	dvd video: emi classic archive DVB 490 4459 *excerpts* vhs video: warner/nvc arts 8573 858013 dvd video: warner/nvc arts 8573 858012
walthamstow 26-29 september 1972	new philharmonia krenz	lp: philips 6500 465

violin concerto in d

walthamstow 26-29 september 1972	new philharmonia krenz	lp: philips 6500 465

WOLFGANG AMADEUS MOZART (1756-1791)
violin concerto no 1 k207

vienna 18-21 may 1955	vienna symphony paumgartner	lp: philips ABL 3147/A00313L lp: philips fontana weltserie 695 035KL lp: philips fontana grandioso 894 105ZKY lp: epic (usa) LC 3230 cd: philips original masters 473 1042

wembley
11-13
april
1962
	london symphony
	davis
		lp: philips AL 3440/SAL 3440/A02253L/
		    835 136AY
		lp: philips universo 6580 009
		lp: philips (usa) PHM 500 236/PHS 900 236
		cd: philips 416 6322/438 3232/438 5642/
		    438 5882/464 7222

moscow 1973	orchestre national de belgique done	lp: melodiya M10 49585 002

violin concerto no 2 k211

vienna 12-13 october 1954	vienna symphony paumgartner	lp: philips ABL 3099/A00258L lp: philips fontana weltserie 695 071KL lp: epic (usa) LC 3157 cd: philips original masters 473 1042

wembley
15-21
may
1964
	london symphony
	davis
		lp: philips AL 3492/SAL 3492/A02378L/
		    835 256LY
		lp: philips (usa) PHM 500 130/PHS 900 130
		cd: philips 416 6322/438 3232/438 5642/
		    438 5882/464 7222

mozart/**violin concerto no 3 k216**

vienna 23-24 november 1953	vienna symphony moralt	lp: philips ABL 3040/A00199L lp: philips classical favourites G05343R lp: philips fontana weltserie 695 048KL lp: eterna 820 132 lp: epic (usa) LC 3060 cd: philips original masters 473 1042 *philips original masters incirrectly names conductor as paumgartner*
prague 1956	prague symphony smetacek	lp: melodiya M10 49585 002
cologne 9 may 1958	wdr orchestra maazel	unpublished radio broadcast *westdeutscher rundfunk*

wembley
27-29
november
1961
	london symphony
	davis
		lp: philips A02224L/835 112AY
		lp: philips diskothek der meister 610 130VR/
		      836 245VZ
		lp: philips (usa) PHM 500 012/PHS 900 012
		cd: philips 412 2502/438 3232/438 5642/
		      438 5882/464 7222

cologne 31 january 1964	wdr orchestra rossi	unpublished radio broadcast *westdeutscher rundfunk*

mozart/**violin concerto no 4 k218**

cologne 23 april 1951	wdr orchestra solti	unpublished radio broadcast *westdeutscher rundfunk*
vienna 23-24 november 1953	vienna symphony moralt	lp: philips ABL 3040/A00199L lp: philips classical favourites G05344R lp: philips fontana weltserie 695 035KL lp: philips fontana grandioso 894 105ZKY lp: eterna 820 132 lp: epic (usa) LC 3060 cd: philips original masters 473 1042 *philips original masters incorrectly names conductor as paumgartner*
stuttgart 2 march 1959	südwestfunk- orchester bour	cd: hänssler CD 93 064 *süddeutscher rundfunk*
würzburg june 1961	bavarian radio orchestra jochum	unpublished radio broadcast *bayerischer rundfunk*

wembley
11-13
april
1962
	london symphony
	davis
		lp: philips AL 3440/SAL 3440/A02253L/
		     835 136AY
		lp: philips universo 6580 009
		lp: philips sequenza 6527 049
		lp: philips (usa) PHM 500 236/PHS 900 236
		cd: philips 416 6322/438 3232/438 5642/
		    438 5882/464 7222

mozart/**violin concerto no 5 k219**

vienna	vienna symphony	lp: philips ABL 3099/A00258L
12-13	paumgartner	lp: philips classical favourites G05345R
october		lp: philips fontana weltserie 695 048KL
1954		lp: epic (usa) LC 3157
		cd: philips original masters 473 1042

munich	bavarian radio	cd: golden melodram GM 40048
9 november	orchestra	
1960	kempe	

wembley	london symphony	lp: philips A02224L/835 112AY/802 781DXY
27-29	davis	lp: philips diskothek der meister 610 128VR/
november		836 240VZ
1961		lp: philips sequenza 6527 049
		lp: philips (usa) PHM 500 012/PHS 900 012
		cd: philips 416 2502/438 3232/438 5642/
		438 5882/464 7222

violin concerto no 7 k271a

vienna	vienna symphony	lp: philips ABL 3147/A00313L
18-21	paumgartner	lp: philips fontana weltserie 695 071KL
may		lp: epic (usa) LC 3230
1955		cd: philips original masters 473 1042

sinfonia concertante for violin and viola k364

hamburg	ndr orchestra	lp: discocorp RR 486
22 january	ackermann	
1955	primrose, viola	

london	london symphony	lp: philips AL 3492/SAL 3492/L02378L/
15-21	davis	835 256LY
may	pelliccia, viola	lp: philips (usa) PHM 500 130/PHS 900 130
1964		cd: philips 438 3232

mozart/**adagio for violin and orchestra k261**
london	london symphony	philips unpublished
15-21	davis	
may		
1964		

wembley	new	lp: philips SAL 3660/802 848LY
5-11	philharmonia	cd: philips 438 3232/438 5642/438 5882
april	leppard	
1967		

rondo for violin and orchestra k373
london	london symphony	philips unpublished
15-21	davis	
may		
1964		

wembley	new	lp: philips SAL 3660/802 848LY
5-11	philharmonia	cd: philips 438 3232/438 5642/438 5882
april	leppard	
1967		

violin sonata no 17 k296
may	klien, piano	lp: philips 412 1411
1982		cd: philips 412 1412

violin sonata no 18 k301
1953	tucker, piano	lp: boston records B 202
		lp: argo RG 109

basel	haskil, piano	lp: philips A00432L/835 103LY/6747 055/
19-20		6768 366/6780 017
november		lp: epic (usa) LC 3602/BC 1034
1958		lp: melodiya S10 13439-13440
		cd: philips 412 2532/442 6252/442 6852

april	klien, piano	lp: philips 412 1411
1981		cd: philips 412 1412

mozart/**violin sonata no 19 k302**
may   klien, piano   lp: philips 412 1411
1981   cd: philips 412 1412

violin sonata no 20 k303
may   klien, piano   lp: philips 412 1411
1982   cd: philips 412 1412

violin sonata no 21 k304
1953   tucker, piano   lp: boston records B 202
                                          lp: argo RG 109

besancon   haskil, piano   lp: discocorp RR 555
18 september   cd: music and arts CD 860
1957   cd: melodram MEL 18001

basel   haskil, piano   lp: philips A00432L/835 103LY/6747 055/
19-20   6768 366/6780 017
november   lp: epic (usa) LC 3602/BC 1034
1958   lp: melodiya S10 13439-13440
                                          cd: philips 412 2532/442 6252/442 6852

violin sonata no 22 k305
september   klien, piano   lp: philips 412 1411
1981   cd: philips 412 1412

violin sonata no 23 k306
september   klien, piano   lp: philips 412 1411
1983   cd: philips 412 1412

mozart/**violin sonata no 24 k376**

basel 19-20 november 1958	haskil, piano	lp: philips A00432L/835 103LY/6747 055/ 6768 366/6780 017 lp: epic (usa) LC 3602/BC 1034 lp: melodiya S10 13439-13440 cd: philips 412 2532/442 6252/442 6852
april 1981	klien, piano	lp: philips 412 1411 cd: philips 412 1412

violin sonata no 25 k377

september 1981	klien, piano	lp: philips 412 1411 cd: philips 412 1412

violin sonata no 26 k378

basel 19-20 november 1958	haskil, piano	lp: philips A00432L/835 103LY/6747 055/ 6768 366/6780 017 lp: epic (usa) LC 3602/BC 1034 lp: melodiya S10 13439-13440 cd: philips 412 2532/442 6252/442 6852
ascona 22 august 1960	haskil, piano	cd: ermitage ERM 112
may 1982	klien, piano	lp: philips 412 1411 cd: philips 412 1412

violin sonata no 27 k379

september 1982	klien, piano	lp: philips 412 1411 cd: philips 412 1412

violin sonata no 28 k380

september 1982	klien, poano	lp: philips 412 1411 cd: philips 412 1412

mozart/**violin sonata no 32 k454**

london 25 march 1946	moore, piano	columbia unpublished

amsterdam
2-5
january
1956
	haskil, piano	lp: philips ABL 3144/A00338L/6747 055/
		      6768 366/6780 017
		lp: epic (usa) LC 3299
		cd: philips 412 4782/442 6252/442 6852/
		      464 7222

besancon 18 september 1957	haskil, piano	lp: discocorp RR 555 cd: music and arts CD 860 cd: melodram MEL 18001
april 1981	klien, piano	lp: philips 412 1411 cd: philips 412 1412

violin sonata no 33 k481

amsterdam october 1959	grumiaux, piano	lp: philips A02078L/802 839LY *violin and piano parts were recorded separately*
september 1983	klien, piano	lp: philips 412 1411 cd: philips 412 1412

violin sonata no 34 k526

amsterdam
2-5
january
1956
	haskil, piano	lp: philips ABL 3144/A00338L/6747 055/
		      6768 366/6780 017
		lp: epic (usa) LC 3299
		cd: philips 412 4782/442 6252/442 6852/
		      464 7222

may 1981	klien, piano	lp: philips 412 1411 cd: philips 412 1412

mozart/**variations on hélas j'ai perdu mon amant, for violin and piano**
september klien, piano lp: philips 412 1411
1981 cd: philips 412 1412

rondo from the haffner serenade, arranged for violin and piano by kreisler
amsterdam hajdu, piano lp: philips A02294L
12 december cd: philips 446 5602
1962

amsterdam hajdu, piano lp: philips 6599 372
12-16
february
1973

minuet from divertimento no 17, arranged for violin and piano by burmester
amsterdam hajdu, piano lp: philips 6599 372-373
12-16 cd: philips 446 6502
february
1973

2 duos for violin and viola k423-424
21-25 pelliccia, viola lp: philips 839 747LY/412 0591
june cd: philips 422 5132/426 8872/454 0232
1968

piano quartet no 2 k493
prades kapell, piano lp: discocorp RR 547
1953 thomas, viola cd: music and arts CD 689
 tortelier, cello

divertimento k563
amsterdam janzer, viola lp: philips SAL 3664/802 803LY
2-6 czako, cello lp: philips (usa) PHS 900 173
june cd: philips 416 4852/422 5132/426 8872/
1967 454 0232/470 9502

six 3-part fugues from bach's wohltemperiertes klavier k404a
le chaux- janzer, viola lp: philips 6500 605
de-fonds czako, cello cd: philips 422 5132/426 8872
12-30 *nos 1, 2 and 3 only*
january cd: philips 416 4852
1973

mozart/**string quintet no 1 k174**

le chaux-	gerecz,	lp: philips 6747 107/412 0571
de-fonds	second violin	cd: philips 416 4862/422 5112/426 8852/
20-28	janzer, viola	456 0552/464 8302/470 9502
may	lesueur, viola	
1973	czako, cello	

string quintet no 2 k406

le chaux-	gerecz,	lp: philips 6747 107
de-fonds	second violin	lp: philips fontana 6570 574
20-28	janzer, viola	cd: philips 416 4862/422 5112/426 8852/
may	lesueur, viola	456 0552/464 8302/470 9502
1973	czako, cello	

string quintet no 3 k515

le chaux-	gerecz,	lp: philips 6747 107
de-fonds	second violin	lp: philips fontana 6570 574
13-17	janzer, viola	cd: philips 416 4862/422 5112/426 8852/
january	lesueur, viola	456 0552/464 8302/470 9502
1973	czako, cello	

string quintet no 4 k516

le chaux-	gerecz,	lp: philips 6747 107/412 0571
de-fonds	second violin	cd: philips 416 4862/422 5112/426 8852/
13-17	janzer, viola	446 2342/456 0582/464 8302/470 9502
january	lesueur, viola	
1973	czako, cello	

string quintet no 5 k593

le chaux-	gerecz,	lp: philips 6747 107/6503 112
de-fonds	second violin	cd: philips 416 4862/422 5112/426 8852/
20-28	janzer, viola	456 0582/464 8302/470 9502
may	lesueur, viola	
1973	czako, cello	

mozart/**string quintet no 6 k614**
le chaux-	gerecz,	lp: philips 6747 107/6503 112
de-fonds	second violin	cd: philips 416 4862/422 5112/426 8852/
20-28	janzer, viola	456 0582/464 8302/470 9502
may	lesueur, viola	
1973	czako, cello	

clarinet quintet k581
1-5	pieterson,	lp: philips 6500 924
october	clarinet	
1974	toyoda,	
	second violin	
	lesueur, viola	
	scholz, cello	

four flute quartets k285, k285a, k285b and k298
16-22	bennett, flute	lp: philips 6500 034
december	janzer, viola	cd: philips 422 5102/426 8842/
1969	czako, cello	442 2992/464 8202

oboe quartet k370
1-5	pierlot, oboe	lp: philips 6500 924
october	lesueur, viola	cd: philips 464 8202
1974	scholz, cello	

MODEST MUSSORGSKY (1839-1881)
gopak from sorotchinsky fair, arranged for violin and piano by dushkin
london	degraux, piano	78: columbia DB 2557/DC 422
6 february		
1947		

PIETRO NARDINI (1722-1793)
violin sonata no 2 in d
amsterdam	hajdu, piano	lp: philips 6500 879
10-12		
june		
1974		

NICCOLO PAGANINI (1782-1840)
violin concerto no 1

monte carlo	monte carlo	lp: philips 6500 411
30 may-	opera orchestra	
8 june	bellugi	
1972		

violin concerto no 4

paris	orchestre	lp: philips ABR 4024/A00741R/A00465L/
8-10	lamoureux	A02426L
november	gallini	lp: philips classical favourites GBL 5576/
1954		G03062L/G05327R
		lp: philips diskothek der meister 836 931VZ
		lp: philips fontana grandioso 894 017ZKY
		lp: epic (usa) LC 3143
		cd: philips original masters 473 1042
		world premiere recording of this re-discovered concerto

monte carlo	monte carlo	lp: philips 6500 411
30 may-	opera orchestra	
8 june	bellugi	
1972		

andante and allegro from violin sonata op 3 no 6

amsterdam	hajdu, piano	lp: philips 6599 372-373
12-16		cd: philips 446 6502
february		
1973		

le streghe/variations on a theme from il noce di benevento

amsterdam	castagnone, piano	lp: philips classical favourites G05372R
14 july		lp: epic (usa) LC 3592
1958		cd: philips 438 5162
		cd: philips original masters 473 1042

variations on di tanti palpiti from rossini's tancredi

amsterdam	castagnone, piano	lp: philips classical favourites GBL 5576/
14 july		G03062L/G05372R
1958		lp: epic (usa) LC 3592
		cd: philips 438 5162
		cd: philips original masters 473 1042

caprice no 14 for solo violin

nice	dvd video: emi classic archive DVB 490 4459
22 january	
1961	

MARIE-THERESE PARADIS (1759-1824)
sicilienne, arranged for violin and piano by dushkin
amsterdam	hajdu, piano	lp: philips 6599 372-373
12-16		cd: philips 446 5602
february		
1973		

GIOVANNI PERGOLESI (1710-1736)
andantino, arranged for violin and piano
amsterdam	hajdu, piano	lp: philips 6599 372-373
12-16		cd: philips 446 6502
february		
1973		

MANUEL PONCE (1882-1948)
estrellita, arranged for violin and piano by heifetz
amsterdam	hajdu, piano	lp: philips 6599 372-373
12-16		cd: philips 446 6502
february		
1973		

MARCEL QUINET (born 1915)
esquisses concertantes pour violon et orchestre
date	orchestre national	lp: decca (belgium) BA 133 198
uncertain	de belgique	
	quinet	

MAURICE RAVEL (1875-1937)
tzigane pour violon et orchestre
paris	orchestre	lp: philips ABL 3126/A00228L
21-22	lamoureux	lp: philips fontana weltserie 695 091KL
june	fournet	lp: epic (usa) LC 3082
1954		cd: philips original masters 473 1042
paris	orchestre	lp: philips SAL 3587/802 708LY/6768 304
march	lamoureux	lp: philips universo 6580 031
1966	rosenthal	lp: philips (usa) PHS 900 195
		cd: philips 416 8862

ravel/**tzigane, version for violin and piano**
london   moore, piano   columbia unpublished
13 june
1945

1953   ulanowsky, piano   lp: boston records (usa) B 203

amsterdam   hajdu, pianp   lp: philips A02294L
december   lp: philips fontana 6570 177
1962   cd: philips 446 6502/454 1432

violin sonata in g
amsterdam   hajdu, piano   lp: philips A02264L/835 174AY
july   lp: philips fontana 6570 177
1962   cd: philips 454 1342
                                                        cd: philips original masters 473 1042

piece en forme de habanera, arranged for violin and piano by cathérine
london   degraux, piano   78: columbia DB 2488/DC 421
5 june
1947

1953   ulanowsky, piano   lp: boston records (usa) B 203

amsterdam   hajdu, piano   lp: philips A02294L
12 december   cd: philips 446 5602/454 1342
1962   cd: philips original masters 473 1042

CAMILLE SAINT-SAENS (1835-1921)
violin concerto no 3

paris	orchestre	lp: philips A00420L/L00465L
21-23	lamoureux	lp: philips classical favourites G05354R
june	fournet	lp: philips fontana weltserie 695 091KL
1954		lp: epic (usa) LC 3399

paris	orchestre	lp: philips AL 3493/SAL 3493/L02375L/
december	lamoureux	835 253LY
1963	rosenthal	lp: philips diskothek der meister 836 931VZ
		lp: philips (usa) PHM 500 061/PHS 900 061

havanaise pour violon et orchestre

paris	orchestre	lp: philips A00420L
26-29	lamoureux	lp: philips classical favourites G05406R
november	fournet	lp: philips fontana weltserie 695 092KL
1956		cd: philips original masters 473 1042

paris	orchestre	lp: philips L02309L/835 184LY/838 127DX/
1-5	lamoureux	839 831GSY/6768 304
april	rosenthal	lp: philips fontana 6570 192
1963		lp: philips fontana grandioso 894 100ZKY

introduction and rondo capriccioso for violin and orchestra

paris	orchestre	45: philips SBF 161
26-29	lamoureux	lp: philips A00420L
november	fournet	lp: epic (usa) LC 3399
1956		cd: philips original masters 473 1042

paris	orchestre	lp: philips L02309L/835 184LY/838 127DX/
1-5	lamoureux	839 831GSY/6768 304
april	rosenthal	lp: philips fontana 6570 192
1963		lp: philips fontana grandioso 894 100ZKY

PABLO DE SARASATE (1844-1908)
zigeunerweisen for violin and piano

amsterdam	hajdu, piano	lp: philips A02294L
12 december		cd: philips 446 6502
1962		cd: philips original masters 473 1042

FRANZ SCHUBERT (1797-1828)
violin sonatina no 1 d384

amsterdam 14-23 july 1958	castagnone, piano	lp: philips A00499L lp: epic (usa) LC 3609 cd: philips 438 5162
1-6 october 1971	veyron-lacroix, piano	lp: philips 6500 341 cd: philips 426 3852
14-18 february 1977	crossley, piano	lp: philips 9500 394

violin sonatina no 2 d385

amsterdam 14-23 july 1958	castagnone, piano	lp: philips A00499L/SBR 6230/S06082R lp: epic (usa) LC 3609 cd: philips 438 5162
1-6 october 1971	veyron-lacroix, piano	lp: philips 6500 341 cd: philips 426 3852
14-18 february 1977	crossley, piano	lp: philips 9500 394

violin sonatina no 3 d408

amsterdam 14-23 july 1958	castagnone, piano	lp: philips A00499L lp: epic (usa) LC 3609 cd: philips 438 5162 *first movement only* lp: philips SBR 6230/S06082R
1-6 october 1971	veyron-lacroix, piano	lp: philips 6500 341 cd: philips 438 3852
14-18 february 1977	crossley, piano	lp: philips 9500 394

schubert/duo in a for violin and piano d574

amsterdam 14-15 july 1958	castagnone, piano	lp: philips A00499L/SBR 6230/S06082R lp: epic (usa) LC 3609 cd: philips 438 5162
1-6 october 1971	veyron-lacroix, piano	lp: philips 6500 341 cd: philips 426 3852
14-18 february 1977	crossley, piano	lp: philips 9500 394

rondo in a for violin and orchestra d438

wembley 5-11 april 1967	new philharmonia leppard	lp: philips SAL 3660/802 848LY

piano quintet d667 "the trout"

23-26 august 1966	haebler, piano janzer, viola czako, cello cazauran, double-bass	lp: philips SAL 3621/802 757LY lp: philips fontana 6570 115

piano trio no 1 d898

crissier 18 december 1972	magaloff, piano fournier, cello	cd: arkadia CD 598/CDHP 598

piano trio no 2 d929

crissier 18 december 1972	magaloff, piano fournier, cello	cd: arkadia CD 598/CDHP 598

string quintet in c d956

1-5 october 1979	gerecz, second violin lesueur, viola czako, cello mermoud, cello	lp: philips 9500 752

schubert/**string trio d471**
february janzer, viola lp: philips SAL 3782/802 905LY
1969 czako, cello cd: philips 422 8362/438 7002

string trio d581
february janzer, viola lp: philips SAL 3782/802 905LY
1969 czako, cello cd: philips 422 8362/438 7002

ave maria, arranged for violin and piano by wilhelmj
amsterdam hajdu, piano lp: philips 6599 372-373
12-16 cd: philips 446 6502
february
1973

ständchen from schwanengesang, arranged for violin and piano
amsterdam hajdu, piano lp: philips 6599 372-373
12-16 cd: philips 446 6502
february
1973

ROBERT SCHUMANN (1810-1856)
träumerei from kinderszenen, arranged for violin and piano
amsterdam hajdu, piano lp: philips 6599 372-373
12-16 cd: philips 446 6502
february
1973

JEAN SIBELIUS (1865-1957)
nocturne from belshazzar's feast, arranged for violin and piano by press
amsterdam hajdu, piano lp: philips 6599 372-373
12-16 cd: philips 446 6502
february
1973

IGOR STRAVINSKY (1882-1971)
violin concerto

cologne	wdr orchestra	cd: archipel ARPCD 0145
16 july	fricsay	*westdeutscher rundfunk*
1953		

amsterdam	concertgebouw	lp: philips SAL 3650/802 785LY
19-21	orchestra	lp: philips sequenza 6527 160
december	bour	lp: philips (usa) PHS 900 194
1966		cd: philips 422 1362

JOHANN SVENDSEN (1840-1911)
romance for violin and orchestra

wembley	new	lp: philips universo 6580 047/412 3721
12-14	philharmonia	
october	de waart	
1970		

KAROL SZYMANOWSKI (1882-1937)
tarantella for violin and piano

london	moore, piano	78: columbia DX 1199
1 june		cd: emi CZS 569 7432
1945		*recording completed on 13 june 1945*

GIUSEPPE TARTINI (1692-1770)
violin sonata in g "devil's trill"

amsterdam	castagnone, piano	45: philips ABE 10090/400 069AE
16-19		lp: philips A00380L
july		lp: epic (usa) LC 3414
1956		cd: philips 438 5162

PIOTR TCHAIKOVSKY (1840-1893)
violin concerto

vienna 29 october- 1 november 1956	vienna symphony leskovich	lp: lp:	philips A00422L epic (usa) LC 3365

amsterdam 11-14 may 1960	concertgebouw orchestra haitink	lp: lp: lp: lp:	philips ABL 3337/AL 3671/SABL 176/ SAL 3671/A02051L/A02821L/835 055AY/ 802 821AY/SBAL 32/SC71AX 403 philips diskothek der meister 610 132VR/ 836 247VZ philips sequenza 6527 067 epic (usa) LC 3745/BC 1109

wembley 1-3 september 1975	new philharmonia krenz	lp:	philips 9500 086

sérénade mélancolique pour violon et orchestre

wembley 12-14 october 1970	new philharmonia de waart	lp: lp:	philips universo 6580 047 philips 412 3721

wembley 1-3 september 1975	new philharmonia krenz	philips unpublished

valse sentimentale in f, arranged for violin and piano by grunes

amsterdam 12-16 february 1973	hajdu, piano	lp: cd:	philips 6599 372-373 philips 446 6502

GEORG PHILIPP TELEMANN (1681-1767)
twelve fantasies for solo violin
3-7   lp: philips 6500 106/9502 010
february
1970

FRANZ VON VECSEY (1893-1935)
valse triste for violin and piano
amsterdam   hajdu, piano   lp: philips 6599 373
12-16   cd: philips 446 6502
february
1973

FRANCESCO MARIA VERACINI (1690-1768)
violin sonata op 1 no 3
amsterdam   hajdu, piano   lp: philips 6500 879
10-15
june
1974

violin sonata op 1 no 7, arranged by castagnone
amsterdam   castagnone, piano   lp: philips A00380L
16-19   lp: epic (usa) LC 3414
july   cd: philips 438 5162
1956

allegro from violin sonata op 1 no 7
amsterdam   hajdu, piano   lp: philips 6599 372
12-16   cd: philips 446 6502
february
1973

largo, arranged by corti
amsterdam   hajdu, piano   lp: philips 6599 373
12-16   cd: philips 446 6502
february
1973

HENRI VIEUXTEMPS (1820-1881)
violin concerto no 4
paris	orchestre	lp: philips SAL 3587/835 708LY
march	lamoureux	lp: philips (france) 6539 045
1966	rosenthal	lp: philips (usa) PHS 900 195
		cd: philips 468 8412

violin concerto no 5
paris	orchestre	lp: philips AL 3493/SAL 3493/A02373L/
december	lamoureux	835 253LY/SBAL 32/SC71AX 503
1963	rosenthal	lp: philips (france) 6539 045
		lp: philips (usa) PHM 500 061/PHS 900 061
		cd: philips 468 8412

ballade and polonaise for violin and piano
8-11	varsi, piano	lp: philips 6500 814
december		lp: musique en wallonie MW 14
1973		cd: philips 468 8412

GIOVANNI BATTISTA VIOTTI (1755-1824)
violin concerto no 22
amsterdam	concertgebouw	lp: philips SAL 3804/839 757LY/6515 002
october	orchestra	
1969	de waart	

TOMASO ANTONIO VITALI (1663-1745)
chaconne in g for violin and piano
amsterdam	castagnone, piano	lp: philips A00380L
16-19		lp: epic (usa) LC 3414
july		cd: philips 438 5162
1956		

ANTONIO VIVALDI (1677-1741)
le 4 stagioni
10-12 november 1978	les solistes romands gerecz, second violin and conductor	lp: philips 9500 613

violin concerto rv271
dresden june 1973	staatskapelle negri	lp: philips 6500 690 lp: eterna 826 495 cd: philips 423 2812

violin concerto rv277
dresden june 1973	staatskapelle negri	lp: philips 6500 690 lp: eterna 826 495 cd: philips 423 2812

violin concerto rv317
dresden june 1973	staatskapelle negri	lp: philips 6500 690 lp: eterna 826 495 cd: philips 423 2812

violin concerto rv356
wembley 1-5 september 1970	new philharmonia de waart	lp: philips 6500 119

violin concerto rv358
dresden june 1973	staatskapelle negri	lp: philips 6500 690 lp: eterna 826 495 cd: philips 423 2812

violin sonata rv31
amsterdam 10-15 june 1974	hajdu, piano	lp: philips 6500 879

sicilienne from violin concerto rv565, arranged for violin and piano
amsterdam 12-15 february 1973	hajdu, piano	lp: philips 6599 372 cd: philips 446 6502

HENRYK WIENIAWSKI (1835-1880)
romance from the second violin concerto
wembley	new	lp: philips universo 6580 047
12-14	philharmonia	lp: philips 412 3721
october	de waart	
1970		

légende pour violon et orchestre
wembley	new	lp: philips universo 6580 047
12-14	philharmonia	lp: philips 412 3721
october	de waart	
1970		

souvenir de moscou, for violin and piano
amsterdam	hajdu, piano	lp: philips 02294L
12 december		cd: philips 446 6502
1962		

EUGENE YSAYE (1858-1931)
reve d'enfant, for violin and piano
8-11	varsi, piano	lp: philips 6500 814
december		lp: musique en wallonie MW 14
1973		

Discographies by Travis & Emery:

Discographies by John Hunt.

1987: From Adam to Webern: the Recordings of von Karajan.

1991: 3 Italian Conductors and 7 Viennese Sopranos: 10 Discographies: Arturo Toscanini, Guido Cantelli, Carlo Maria Giulini, Elisabeth Schwarzkopf, Irmgard Seefried, Elisabeth Gruemmer, Sena Jurinac, Hilde Gueden, Lisa Della Casa, Rita Streich.

1992: Mid-Century Conductors and More Viennese Singers: 10 Discographies: Karl Boehm, Victor De Sabata, Hans Knappertsbusch, Tullio Serafin, Clemens Krauss, Anton Dermota, Leonie Rysanek, Eberhard Waechter, Maria Reining, Erich Kunz.

1993: More 20th Century Conductors: 7 Discographies: Eugen Jochum, Ferenc Fricsay, Carl Schuricht, Felix Weingartner, Josef Krips, Otto Klemperer, Erich Kleiber.

1994: Giants of the Keyboard: 6 Discographies: Wilhelm Kempff, Walter Gieseking, Edwin Fischer, Clara Haskil, Wilhelm Backhaus, Artur Schnabel.

1994: Six Wagnerian Sopranos: 6 Discographies: Frieda Leider, Kirsten Flagstad, Astrid Varnay, Martha Moedl, Birgit Nilsson, Gwyneth Jones.

1995: Musical Knights: 6 Discographies: Henry Wood, Thomas Beecham, Adrian Boult, John Barbirolli, Reginald Goodall, Malcolm Sargent.

1995: A Notable Quartet: 4 Discographies: Gundula Janowitz, Christa Ludwig, Nicolai Gedda, Dietrich Fischer-Dieskau.

1996: The Post-War German Tradition: 5 Discographies: Rudolf Kempe, Joseph Keilberth, Wolfgang Sawallisch, Rafael Kubelik, Andre Cluytens.

1996: Teachers and Pupils: 7 Discographies: Elisabeth Schwarzkopf, Maria Ivoguen, Maria Cebotari, Meta Seinemeyer, Ljuba Welitsch, Rita Streich, Erna Berger.

1996: Tenors in a Lyric Tradition: 3 Discographies: Peter Anders, Walther Ludwig, Fritz Wunderlich.

1997: The Lyric Baritone: 5 Discographies: Hans Reinmar, Gerhard Hüsch, Josef Metternich, Hermann Uhde, Eberhard Wächter.

1997: Hungarians in Exile: 3 Discographies: Fritz Reiner, Antal Dorati, George Szell.

1997: The Art of the Diva: 3 Discographies: Claudia Muzio, Maria Callas, Magda Olivero.

1997: Metropolitan Sopranos: 4 Discographies: Rosa Ponselle, Eleanor Steber, Zinka Milanov, Leontyne Price.

1997: Back From The Shadows: 4 Discographies: Willem Mengelberg, Dimitri Mitropoulos, Hermann Abendroth, Eduard Van Beinum.

1997: More Musical Knights: 4 Discographies: Hamilton Harty, Charles Mackerras, Simon Rattle, John Pritchard.

1998: Conductors On The Yellow Label: 8 Discographies: Fritz Lehmann, Ferdinand Leitner, Ferenc Fricsay, Eugen Jochum, Leopold Ludwig, Artur Rother, Franz Konwitschny, Igor Markevitch.

1998: More Giants of the Keyboard: 5 Discographies: Claudio Arrau, Gyorgy Cziffra, Vladimir Horowitz, Dinu Lipatti, Artur Rubinstein.

1998: Mezzos and Contraltos: 5 Discographies: Janet Baker, Margarete Klose, Kathleen Ferrier, Giulietta Simionato, Elisabeth Höngen.
1999: The Furtwängler Sound Sixth Edition: Discography and Concert Listing.
1999: The Great Dictators: 3 Discographies: Evgeny Mravinsky, Artur Rodzinski, Sergiu Celibidache.
1999: Sviatoslav Richter: Pianist of the Century: Discography.
2000: Philharmonic Autocrat 1: Discography of: Herbert Von Karajan [Third Edition].
2000: Wiener Philharmoniker 1 - Vienna Philharmonic & Vienna State Opera Orchestras: Disc. Part 1 1905-1954.
2000: Wiener Philharmoniker 2 - Vienna Philharmonic & Vienna State Opera Orchestras: Disc. Part 2 1954-1989.
2001: Gramophone Stalwarts: 3 Separate Discographies: Bruno Walter, Erich Leinsdorf, Georg Solti.
2001: Singers of the Third Reich: 5 Discographies: Helge Roswaenge, Tiana Lemnitz, Franz Völker, Maria Müller, Max Lorenz.
2001: Philharmonic Autocrat 2: Concert Register of Herbert Von Karajan Second Edition.
2002: Sächsische Staatskapelle Dresden: Complete Discography.
2002: Carlo Maria Giulini: Discography and Concert Register.
2002: Pianists For The Connoisseur: 6 Discographies: Arturo Benedetti Michelangeli, Alfred Cortot, Alexis Weissenberg, Clifford Curzon, Solomon, Elly Ney.
2003: Singers on the Yellow Label: 7 Discographies: Maria Stader, Elfriede Trötschel, Annelies Kupper, Wolfgang Windgassen, Ernst Häfliger, Josef Greindl, Kim Borg.
2003: A Gallic Trio: 3 Discographies: Charles Münch, Paul Paray, Pierre Monteux.
2004: Antal Dorati 1906-1988: Discography and Concert Register.
2004: Columbia 33CX Label Discography.
2004: Great Violinists: 3 Discographies: David Oistrakh, Wolfgang Schneiderhan, Arthur Grumiaux.
2006: Leopold Stokowski: Second Edition of the Discography.
2006: Wagner Im Festspielhaus: Discography of the Bayreuth Festival.
2006: Her Master's Voice: Concert Register and Discography of Dame Elisabeth Schwarzkopf [Third Edition].
2007: Hans Knappertsbusch: Kna: Concert Register and Discography of Hans Knappertsbusch, 1888-1965. Second Edition.
2008: Philips Minigroove: Second Extended Version of the European Discography.
2009: American Classics: The Discographies of Leonard Bernstein and Eugene Ormandy.

Discography by Stephen J. Pettitt, edited by John Hunt:
1987: Philharmonia Orchestra: Complete Discography 1945-1987

Available from: Travis & Emery at 17 Cecil Court, London, UK. (+44) 20 7 240 2129. email on sales@travis-and-emery.com .

© Travis & Emery 2009

Music and Books published by Travis & Emery Music Bookshop:

Anon.: Hymnarium Sarisburense, cum Rubris et Notis Musicus
Agricola, Johann Friedrich from Tosi: Anleitung zur Singkunst. (Faksimile 1757)
Bach, C.P.E.: edited W. Emery: Nekrolog or Obituary Notice of J.S. Bach.
Bateson, Naomi Judith: Alcock of Salisbury
Bathe, William: A Briefe Introduction to the Skill of Song
Bax, Arnold: Symphony #5, Arranged for Piano Four Hands by Walter Emery
Burney, Charles: The Present State of Music in France and Italy
Burney, Charles: The Present State of Music in Germany, The Netherlands …
Burney, Charles: An Account of the Musical Performances … Handel
Burney, Karl: Nachricht von Georg Friedrich Handel's Lebensumstanden.
Burns, Robert (jnr): The Caledonian Musical Museum (1810 volume)
Cobbett, W.W.: Cobbett's Cyclopedic Survey of Chamber Music. (2 vols.)
Corrette, Michel: Le Maitre de Clavecin
Crimp, Bryan: Dear Mr. Rosenthal … Dear Mr. Gaisberg …
Crimp, Bryan: Solo: The Biography of Solomon
d'Indy, Vincent: Beethoven: Biographie Critique
d'Indy, Vincent: Beethoven: A Critical Biography
d'Indy, Vincent: César Franck (in French)
Fischhof, Joseph: Versuch einer Geschichte des Clavierbaues
Frescobaldi, Girolamo: D'Arie Musicali per Cantarsi. Primo Libro & Secondo Libro.
Geminiani, Francesco: The Art of Playing the Violin.
Handel; Purcell; Boyce; Green et al: Calliope or English Harmony: Volume First.
Hawkins, John: A General History of the Science and Practice of Music (5 vols.)
Herbert-Caesari, Edgar: The Science and Sensations of Vocal Tone
Herbert-Caesari, Edgar: Vocal Truth
Hopkins and Rimboult: The Organ. Its History and Construction.
Hunt, John: some 40 discographies – see list of discographies
Isaacs, Lewis: Hänsel and Gretel. A Guide to Humperdinck's Opera.
Isaacs, Lewis: Königskinder (Royal Children) A Guide to Humperdinck's Opera.
Lacassagne, M. l'Abbé Joseph : Traité Général des élémens du Chant.
Lascelles (née Catley), Anne: The Life of Miss Anne Catley.
Mainwaring, John: Memoirs of the Life of the Late George Frederic Handel
Malcolm, Alexander: A Treaty of Music: Speculative, Practical and Historical
Marx, Adolph Bernhard: Die Kunst des Gesanges, Theoretisch-Practisch
May, Florence: The Life of Brahms
Mellers, Wilfrid: Angels of the Night: Popular Female Singers of Our Time
Mellers, Wilfrid: Bach and the Dance of God

Travis & Emery Music Bookshop
17 Cecil Court, London, WC2N 4EZ, United Kingdom.
Tel. (+44) 20 7240 2129

Music and Books published by Travis & Emery Music Bookshop:

Mellers, Wilfrid: Beethoven and the Voice of God
Mellers, Wilfrid: Caliban Reborn - Renewal in Twentieth Century Music
Mellers, Wilfrid: François Couperin and the French Classical Tradition
Mellers, Wilfrid: Harmonious Meeting
Mellers, Wilfrid: Le Jardin Retrouvé, The Music of Frederic Mompou
Mellers, Wilfrid: Music and Society, England and the European Tradition
Mellers, Wilfrid: Music in a New Found Land: … ... American Music
Mellers, Wilfrid: Romanticism and the Twentieth Century (from 1800)
Mellers, Wilfrid: The Masks of Orpheus: …… the Story of European Music.
Mellers, Wilfrid: The Sonata Principle (from c. 1750)
Mellers, Wilfrid: Vaughan Williams and the Vision of Albion
Panchianio, Cattuffio: Rutzvanscad Il Giovine.
Pearce, Charles: Sims Reeves, Fifty Years of Music in England.
Pettitt, Stephen: Philharmonia Orchestra: Complete Discography 1945-1987
Playford, John: An Introduction to the Skill of Musick.
Purcell, Henry et al: Harmonia Sacra … The First Book, (1726)
Purcell, Henry et al: Harmonia Sacra … Book II (1726)
Quantz, Johann: Versuch einer Anweisung die Flöte traversiere zu spielen.
Rameau, Jean-Philippe: Code de Musique Pratique, ou Methodes.
Rastall, Richard: The Notation of Western Music.
Rimbault, Edward: The Pianoforte, Its Origins, Progress, and Construction.
Rousseau, Jean Jacques: Dictionnaire de Musique
Rubinstein, Anton : Guide to the proper use of the Pianoforte Pedals.
Sainsbury, John S.: Dictionary of Musicians. Vol. 1. (1825). 2 vols.
Simpson, Christopher: A Compendium of Practical Musick in Five Parts
Spohr, Louis: Autobiography
Spohr, Louis: Grand Violin School
Tans'ur, William: A New Musical Grammar; or The Harmonical Spectator
Terry, Charles Sanford: Four-Part Chorals of J.S. Bach. (German & English)
Terry, Charles Sanford: Joh. Seb. Bach, Cantata Texts, Sacred and Secular.
Terry, Charles Sanford: The Origins of the Family of Bach Musicians.
Tosi, Pierfrancesco: Opinioni de' Cantori Antichi, e Moderni
Van der Straeten, Edmund: History of the Violoncello, The Viol da Gamba …
Van der Straeten, Edmund: History of the Violin, Its Ancestors… (2 vols.)
Walther, J. G.: Musicalisches Lexikon ober Musicalische Bibliothec (1732)

Travis & Emery Music Bookshop
17 Cecil Court, London, WC2N 4EZ, United Kingdom.
Tel. (+44) 20 7240 2129

© Travis & Emery 2009

www.ingramcontent.com/pod-product-compliance
Lightning Source LLC
Chambersburg PA
CBHW070825250426
43671CB00036B/2070